An Imperial Disaster

An Imperial Disaster

THE BENGAL CYCLONE OF 1876

Benjamin Kingsbury

SPEAKING
TIGER

SPEAKING TIGER PUBLISHING PVT. LTD
4381/4, Ansari Road, Daryaganj
New Delhi – 110002

First published in the United Kingdom by
C. Hurst & Co. (Publishers) Ltd., 2018

First published in India by Speaking Tiger, 2019
Copyright © Benjamin Kingsbury, 2018

This edition for sale in South Asia only

ISBN:978-93-88326-77-3
eISBN:978-93-88326-78-0

10 9 8 7 6 5 4 3 2 1

Printed at Sanat Printers, Kundli

For my parents
John Kingsbury and Sharon Scott

There are blows in life so hard ... I don't know!
Blows as if from the hatred of God; as if before them,
the deep waters of everything lived through
were backed up in the soul ...

César Vallejo

CONTENTS

PREFACE

On a winter's day in 1874, during his annual tour of the district, the collector of Bakarganj, Henry Beveridge, stopped at a village on the bank of the Tetulia river. Kachua had once been the seat of the rajas of Chandradwip, the most powerful landowning family of Bakarganj in Mughal times; but the fortunes of the family, and of their ancestral estate, had taken a turn after the desolation of Bakarganj by a cyclone and storm-wave in 1584.

'In the twenty-ninth year of the present reign,' the Mughal historian Abul Fazl wrote, 'one afternoon at three o'clock, there was a terrible inundation which deluged the whole Sarkar [district]. The Rajah was at an entertainment, from which he embarked in a boat; his son, Parmanand Roy, with a few others climbed to the top of a Hindoo temple, and the merchants betook themselves to a high loft. It blew a hurricane, with thunder and lightning, for five hours, during which time the sea was greatly agitated. The houses and boats were swallowed up, nothing remaining but the loft and the Hindoo temple on the height.'

This great storm, about which nothing else is known, might on its own have been enough to force the rajas of Chandradwip to leave Kachua and settle in the safer north. There was also a tradition that they left because of a change in the course of the river (perhaps itself a result of the storm-wave) that caused a large part of their land to be washed away. But it was not only the forces of nature that the rajas and their subjects had to contend with. The seaboard of Bengal was also, in these years, under attack from Portuguese pirates based at Chittagong, mercenaries of the king of Arakan. 'They swept the sea coast,' the French traveller François Bernier wrote, 'seizing as slaves both men and women, small and great, perpetrating strange cruelties, and burning all they could not carry away.' By the mid-seventeenth century the southern part of Bengal had been almost entirely depopulated.

The Arakanese (or 'Maghs') were defeated by the Mughal governor Shaista Khan in 1666, and settlement slowly began to move south again. But when the British took control of Bengal a hundred years later the seaboard of Bakarganj was still covered by forest, and the islands in the estuary were only sparsely populated. 'This part of the Country', reads an inscription on James Rennell's 1776 map of Bengal, 'has been Deserted on Account of the Ravages of the Muggs.'

By the 1870s much of the forest had been cut down, and the south of Bakarganj had been repopulated. At the time of Beveridge's visit in 1874 Kachua was a village like any other in the district—a scattering of mat and thatch homesteads surrounded by orchards, paddy fields, and tanks. All that remained of the Chandradwip rajas was a deserted temple on a mound overlooking the river, and further inland several vaulted chambers of strong masonry: the ruins of the raja's palace.

It would be only two years until the temple and palace, and everybody living around them, would once again be swallowed up by the sea.

⁂

This book tells the story of the Bengal cyclone of 1876. The storm came on the night of 31 October. It was a full moon, and the tides were at their peak; the great rivers of eastern Bengal were flowing high and fast to the sea. In the early hours of the morning the inhabitants of the coast and islands were overtaken by an immense wave from the Bay of Bengal—a wall of water that reached a height of 40 feet in some places. The wave swept away everything in its path; around 215,000 people were drowned. At least another 100,000 died in the cholera epidemic and famine that followed. It was the worst calamity of its kind in recorded history.

Such events are often described as 'natural disasters'. The expression is not an unreasonable one: the extreme natural forces at work are impossible to overlook. Yet a focus on extreme forces tends to obscure the less spectacular, though equally important, human elements of calamity. It becomes possible to think of disasters as existing beyond human control or responsibility, isolated events without any connection to the processes of historical change. This book treats the Bengal cyclone as a human and historical event. It suggests that this was not simply a 'natural' disaster, but one shaped by all-too-human patterns of exploitation and inequality—by divisions within Bengali society, and by the great disparities of political and economic power that characterised British rule in India.

The districts affected by the cyclone were among the most isolated in the empire. Bakarganj and Noakhali had been left untouched by the railway and telegraph; it was a journey of several days by boat from their headquarters towns to the nearest city. Chittagong had its port, but was still a long way from the provincial (and imperial) capital of Calcutta. The isolation of the islands in the Meghna estuary, divided between Bakarganj and Noakhali, was even more extreme: for much of the year they were cut off from the mainland by the estuary's massive rivers. Even today the journey to Sandwip and Hatia is a slow and uncertain one.

Many of the cyclone's victims were recent migrants to the coast. For fifty years the government had been trying to increase its land revenue by encouraging the settlement of newly-formed land in the estuary. It had also encouraged the clearance and settlement of the Bakarganj Sundarbans, the mangrove forest that offered the only defence against the storm-waves of the Bay of Bengal. There were plenty of people ready to move to this dangerous new frontier: the destruction of the estuary's main industries, textiles and salt, had thrown thousands out of work, and the population of the delta was steadily increasing. The landlords and their rent-receiving intermediaries prospered through this 'reclamation' of forest and alluvial land; their tenants, the poorest cultivators and labourers, were left exposed to the sea.

Poor people living in remote places are easy to forget. Just six months after the cyclone, at a time when many of its victims were still without adequate food or shelter, a writer in a popular science magazine observed that the calamity had already been forgotten by the outside world. 'No more convincing proof could be given of the headlong pace of our modern life, or of the thoughtlessness of our age, than the fact that ... hardly a word is said of the fearfully destructive cyclone which, on the 31st of October, 1876, swept over the Delta of the Ganges. Even in the Queen's last speech from the throne, there is not so much as a simple mention of that disastrous event, whereby a quarter of a million of British subjects in India were destroyed.'

If the Bengal cyclone has remained a forgotten disaster it is not because of a lack of records. The proceedings of the government of Bengal, held at the College Street branch of the West Bengal State Archives in Calcutta, contain hundreds of pages of documents on the cyclone and its aftermath. Those pages tell much of the story disclosed here: the horrors of the storm-wave, the implementation of Sir Richard Temple's patently inadequate relief policy, the terrible outbreak of cholera that followed the storm, and the efforts of Romesh Dutt—future economic nationalist and critic of British rule in India—to avert famine on the island of Dakhin Shahbazpur. The newspapers of Calcutta and small-town Bengal add the voices of a middle-class public that was forthright in its criticisms of the government, yet reluctant to offer any help to the victims itself.

The cyclone must have provided material for many poems, songs, and stories, but few of these would have been written down. One poem that has been preserved, Nagendra Ray's *Pabaner Otyachar* (The Terror of a Storm), makes up the epilogue of this book. The poem is organised around a trial of the gods; the accuser is a young woman, a prostitute, from Dakhin Shahbazpur. The woman stands in for humanity, helpless and bewildered in the face of an inexplicable calamity. She recounts her suffering and the suffering of others, and asks for justice. It seemed appropriate to end with this reminder that for most people living along the coast, disasters were—and are—acts not of people, or of nature, but of God.

There are good reasons now to revisit the cyclone of 1876. The destruction caused by cyclones and storm-waves along the coast of eastern Bengal (present-day Bangladesh) has been greater than anywhere else in the world, and many of the problems that prefigure disaster—overpopulation, unemployment, landlessness, corruption, illiteracy, indebtedness, official indifference—have outlasted British rule. There is also the prospect of rising sea levels and stronger, more frequent storms. Already climate change is being blamed for disasters along the coast of Bangladesh. Yet terrible storms are nothing new, and the sad stories of people displaced by the estuary's rivers have been told before. Change, on the coast, is constant and inescapable: climate change is only one problem among many, inseparable from all the rest.

'The island of Maunpoora', the surveyor Robert Smart wrote in the 1860s, 'is fast disappearing, and will soon be submerged beneath the waves.' The island is still there today. Its future is uncertain. But the future is an abstraction: it offers no material for thought or action. The past, in its particularity, might be a better place to begin.

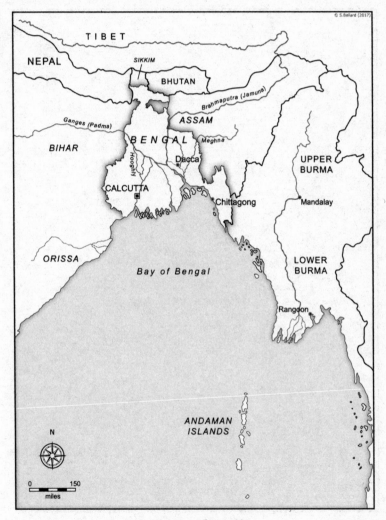

The Bay of Bengal

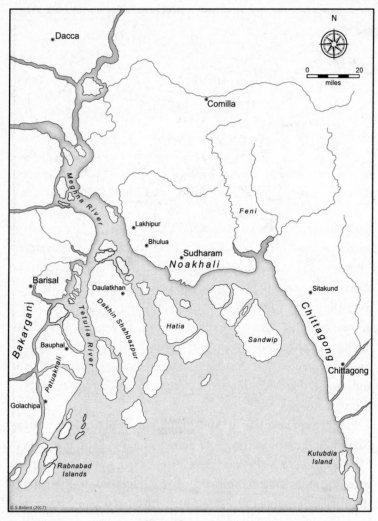

The Meghna Estuary

1

THE ESTUARY

Early in December 1850 Joseph Hooker left Sylhet, in the north-eastern corner of Bengal, for the south-eastern district of Chittagong. He was travelling by boat: it was the most common form of transport in the delta. Just below Dacca, still a long way from the sea, the first signs of the tide appeared. A few days later he reached the estuary of the Meghna. The river opened out further, and to the discomfort of his fresh-water boatmen a long swell came rolling in. On the horizon were low islands of sand and mud; distorted by refraction, they flickered 'as if seen through smoke'.

Hooker spent a day at Sudharam, the headquarters town of Noakhali, before setting off across the head of the bay to Chittagong. He had been given a large boat and a crew experienced in navigating the estuary: it was a full moon, the time of the tidal bore, and the voyage was considered dangerous. The boatmen put out with the tide at three in the morning. Two hours later they pulled into a creek on the island of Siddhi. The water drained away, leaving the boat resting on the creekbed. 'As far as the eye could reach,' Hooker wrote, 'all was a glistening oozy mud, except the bleak level surface of the islands, on which neither shrub nor tree grew.'

All morning they waited in the empty creek. Then, at two in the afternoon, they heard a roaring sound in the distance. The birds feeding on the sandbanks sprang into the air; a long white line appeared on the horizon. This was the bore: the tidal wave that came up the estuary at every full and new moon, 15 or 20 feet high. If the boat had been in the open channel it would have been swamped. Safely in the creek, an hour later it was afloat—but that evening it was grounded again, waiting out another bore. The wave came in the middle of the night, but the boatmen were ready: they seemed, Hooker thought, to waken 'by instinct' before it arrived.

The bore wasn't the only difficulty the estuary's boatmen had to face. Summer storms and monsoon rains made the rivers rough and dangerous for most of the year; settled weather could be expected only in the cooler months, from November to February. In all seasons there was the risk of grounding on one of the constantly-shifting sandbanks and shoals. The flat-bottomed country boats of the estuary drew only a foot or two of water, but if there was a fair wind one of the crew would always be stationed at the bow with a bamboo pole, testing the depth of the stream.

Every journey depended on the direction of the tide: only a steamer could make any headway against it. A single short trip might take several different tides—with the ebb down one arm of a creek, with the flood up another. If the tide was going in the wrong direction the only thing to do was to drop anchor and wait for it to turn. 'It is fatiguing', Henry Beveridge wrote, 'to find that you cannot reach a place only ten miles off on the map in less than eight or nine hours, and that if wind and tide be against you, you may not reach it in less than a day and a half.'

When the boatmen got beyond the influence of the tides they worked to the limits of physical endurance. The surveyor Francis

Buchanan, travelling downriver to Noakhali in May 1798, himself suffering from the heat, left a description of their labours in his journal. 'I know no Europeans, who undergo such long continued labour with so little rest or nourishment, as the boatmen of Bengal do. Mine had wrought from seven in the morning to eleven at night, without eating; nor was their exertion considered as extraordinary.'

The boatmen's earnings were far from proportionate to their exertion. Many could not make a living year-round on the rivers, and had to work as labourers during the harvest season. Their health, too, seems to have been poor, even by the standards of the time. Henry Beveridge noticed that they suffered especially badly from skin diseases, 'the soles of their feet being often drilled with holes like a sponge'. They also suffered from fever and dysentery: the sudden death of a boatman in 'a paroxysm of fever and ague' was no cause for surprise.

To proof themselves against the weather and the pain of their labour the boatmen smoked strong Rajshahi ganja and added handfuls of red chilli to their meals. Before they went out on the water they chanted a verse to Badar, a Muslim saint buried at Chittagong whose spirit watched over the rivers. And when they were on the water they had all their experience and instinct to draw on. Even so, accidents were common. The boatmen didn't like going out during the bore or in bad weather, but often they had no choice. And in their ramshackle, easily flooded settlements along the banks of the rivers and creeks, they were even at risk on land.

Disaster, for the boatmen of the Meghna estuary, was only the shadow of poverty: whether on the water or off it, when a cyclone came they would be the first to die.

෧෪

The estuary had been formed by the combined waters of two great rivers: the Ganges (known in eastern Bengal as the Padma) and the Brahmaputra (known as the Jamuna). These rivers were continually shifting their courses. It was James Rennell who made the first reliable survey of Bengal in the 1760s. At this time the Brahmaputra and the much smaller Meghna joined the Ganges south of Lakhipur, a port town in Noakhali. After the great flood of 1787 the Brahmaputra changed course dramatically, moving far to the west to join the Ganges in Faridpur. A comparison between Rennell's survey and the revenue survey of the 1860s shows that the combined river, which took its name from the Meghna, was moving steadily to the east. The only thing that hadn't changed was the combined river's size and power: it was, Rennell thought, 'a body of fresh running water, hardly to be equalled in the old hemisphere, and, perhaps, not exceeded in the new'.

On the western side of the big river, dipping into the Bay of Bengal, was the mainland of Bakarganj: an alluvial formation, completely flat, cut up in all directions by rivers and creeks. To the east was the Noakhali mainland, also flat and alluvial but with fewer waterways. South-east of Noakhali was the hilly district of Chittagong, fringed along its seaward edge by a narrow, fertile plain. These three districts formed a half-circle around a gulf crowded with islands. A few of the islands—Dakhin Shahbazpur, Hatia, Sandwip—were large and well established. Others, some so new they hadn't yet been named, were smaller and in a state of flux. The smaller islands, along with the shoals, sandbanks, and other newly-formed lands, were known as chars. Many of the chars disappeared from sight at high tide, only to be revealed again by the ebb: it was a world in which the ordinary boundaries between land and water hardly existed.

The rivers of the estuary had extraordinary powers of creation and destruction. 'In places where the current is remarkably rapid, or the soil uncommonly loose,' Rennell wrote, 'such tracts are swept away in the course of one season, as would astonish those who have not been eyewitnesses to the magnitude and force of these mighty streams.' But what the rivers took with one hand they returned with the other. Soil cut away from the steep bank of a channel was swept downstream and left as a shelving bank on the other side; islands 4 or 5 miles long came up in mid-channel within a few seasons, forming around a piece of collapsed riverbank, a fallen tree, or even a sunken boat. 'Places that are now Channels, were a few Years back high Sands', Robert Knox wrote in the field book of his 1803 survey of the estuary. 'And Sands and low islands now ... were formerly Channels.'

Every year cyclones came in from the Bay of Bengal at the beginning and end of the south-west monsoon, from May to June and October to November. These storms had as great an effect on the shape of the estuary as the currents and tides. Heavy swells stirred up the mudflats at the head of the bay and carried their silt back onto the land. The storm-waves that sometimes accompanied the cyclones broke over the islands and swept several miles inland. Joseph Hooker thought that this explained the slight elevation of the Noakhali coast and islands. Usually the waves left only a fine layer of sand and silt as they receded; but the wave of 1848, Hooker's host in Noakhali told him, had covered Sandwip with a deposit of sediment 6 inches deep.

It was not just a case of land being taken from one place and moved to another. There was also growth. As the rivers emptied into the sea they released the loads they had carried down from the northern mountains and plains. Himalayan slopes were reincarnated as piles of silt in the Bay of Bengal; a glass dipped into the water would yield a quarter part of mud. Rennell thought that despite the action of the currents and tides, the land was gaining on the sea. 'The sand and mud banks extend twenty miles off some of the islands in the mouths of the Ganges and Burrampooter, and in many places rise within a few feet of the surface.' These submerged lands, he predicted, would eventually form a new frontier of settlement in the estuary. 'Some future generation will probably see these banks rise above water, and succeeding ones possess and cultivate them!'

Rennell was a careful observer. The revenue survey of the 1860s showed that large amounts of land had been created on the Bakarganj side of the estuary in the last hundred years. In Rennell's time Dakhin Shahbazpur had been separated from the mainland by the main channel of the Meghna, which ran out to sea past an archipelago of small islands. Forty years later Knox described the signs of growth. 'Many of the islands between Deccan Shabezpoor and the Sunderbund side [the Bakarganj mainland] are seemingly newly formed and some are in a state of formation, none of which are yet inhabited, but all covered with Grass and Buffaloes.' By the time of the revenue survey these islands had expanded and attached themselves to Dakhin Shahbazpur. The main channel of the river had moved from the western side of the island to its east. A vast plain of new land had formed in the south, and new islands had come up further out in the estuary. 'The islands south-east of Don Manik's islands,' one surveyor wrote, 'not marked at all in old maps, are rapidly approaching a state in which vegetation will exist on them, while others, somewhat older, are already inhabited.'

There had been a similar transformation on the Noakhali side of the estuary. According to tradition, the islands of Sandwip and Hatia had once been so close to each other that a person calling out from one could be heard on the other. Sandwip had not changed much since the eighteenth century, but Hatia had become an entirely different landform—all it had kept was its name. A survey from the 1830s shows that even then it had moved so far to the west that it only overlapped by a quarter with the Hatia of Rennell's survey. The tides had done most of the work of erosion and deposition, cutting away the eastern side of the island and rebuilding it on the west. At the same time the mainland of Noakhali was building into the Bay of Bengal, char following char like the pieces of a jigsaw. In the eighteenth century the Noakhali coast had passed just south of Sudharam; by 1876 the town was 8 miles from the coast, everything in between being newly-formed land.

In the years before 1876 the rivers had created a new frontier: a fringe of alluvial land around the mainland and existing islands, and many new islands too. It was an unstable frontier, always shifting, subject to the action of the rivers from the north and the Bay of Bengal from the south. Rennell, when he saw the new land coming up, had predicted that it would soon be cultivated. But who would settle this frontier, and on what terms? The opportunities for profit were great—but so were the dangers.

❧

By 1876 it could be written of Noakhali that 'no manufactures worthy of the name are carried on in the district, and there is no manufacturing class'. It was said that the largest workshop in Bakarganj was the Barisal jail. The mainstay of both districts was agriculture. According to the 1872 census three quarters of the men of Noakhali, and two thirds of Bakarganj, worked in the fields. Nearly all of the women worked at home.

The sources of wealth in these districts had once been much wider. When European trading companies arrived in Bengal in the seventeenth century the province had been renowned for its cotton cloth. Its fine muslins were exported all over the world, and a large quantity of coarser cloth was made for the home market. It wasn't only the merchants and weavers who prospered: every stage of the manufacture, from the cultivation of the cotton to its spinning and bleaching, gave employment to the people of the province.

At first the servants of the British East India Company were just another band of opportunistic traders. Following the established pattern, they advanced money to local merchants, who in turn advanced money to the weavers. In Noakhali they traded from stations at Jugdia, near the mouth of the Feni river; at Kalyandi, further inland; and at Lakhipur, on the coast. But the Company's rise to political supremacy in the 1760s brought big changes to the textile industry. The rules of the market were replaced by the rule of superior force. Merchants working for the Company could no longer expect market rates for their services, and the prices paid to the weavers were hardly enough to meet their costs. The industry continued to grow, but the share of its profits in the hands of the merchants and weavers diminished.

The weavers rented land for their food crops and cotton as well as for their houses and workshops. This meant that along with the extortions of the Company's commercial branch, carried out by the merchants, they had to face the extortions of its land revenue branch, carried out by the tax-collecting zamindars. The zamindars added their own charges—a loom tax on Dakhin Shahbazpur, for instance—to the Company's already high revenue demands. Like the merchants, they were ready to use force against the weavers to ensure their compliance.

The weavers found themselves caught in the pincers of the new administration. Their ability to pay taxes was limited by the low prices they got for their cloth, and their ability to fall back on agriculture was limited by the small size of their holdings. Francis Buchanan saw that most families in Noakhali would struggle to make a living from their land alone. 'In this part of the Country there is hardly such a thing as a farmer. Every Artificer, Boatman, Labourer or servant rents a small piece of ground: he pays his rent, Cloathing, and religious or festival expenses by the wages he gets, and by his wife's spinning; and he has the produce of his Ground for food, and for the raw materials of Cloathing.' The conditions of the textile trade might have been miserable: but for artificers employed by the Company in weaving cloth, its loss would mean the loss of their subsistence.

The invention of the spinning mule in Britain in the late eighteenth century marked the beginning of the end for Bengal's cotton trade. The British manufacturers had steam power and new machines, and were protected by a 75 per cent duty on imports. They quickly shut Bengal out of what had been its largest export market. The highly-skilled weavers of Dacca were the first to suffer: the number of muslins sent from the city fell year by year until the commercial residency was finally closed in 1817. And there was worse to come. India had been opened to free trade in 1813, and in the 1820s British thread and fabrics began to pour into Bengal. The machine-made goods, subject only to a nominal duty, undersold the local products; and the spinners and weavers lost most of their home market too. 'The foreign manufacturer', a sympathetic British author wrote, 'employed the arm of political injustice to keep down and ultimately strangle a competitor with whom he could not have competed on equal terms.'

Dacca's population fell from 200,000 in 1800 to 68,000 in 1838. James Taylor, a surgeon working in the city, described the miserable circumstances of those who remained. 'Many families who were formerly in a state of affluence are now reduced to comparative poverty, while the majority of people belonging to the lower classes, are from want of work in a very destitute condition, and are glad to procure any employment, however unsuited to their previous habits, to enable them to earn a subsistence for themselves and their families.' There are no migration statistics to show the destinations of those who left Dacca in these years. Some would have gone to the fast-growing metropolis of Calcutta, by now Bengal's only real city. But others would have drifted south to labour on the forest estates of the Bakarganj Sundarbans or the seaboard chars of Noakhali—both of which, in the 1820s and 1830s, were being populated as part of a state-sponsored drive to increase the land revenue.

The effects of industrial decline were also felt directly in Noakhali. The area around Lakhipur was second only to Dacca in the value of textiles bought by the Company; the cloth trade of the district as a whole was worth about Rs. 12,000,000 a year. Noakhali was a producer of medium-quality and coarse cloth, and its trade didn't fall off as quickly as Dacca's; but by the end of the 1820s its trading stations had also closed. Even then the Jugis, a weaving caste, kept the local markets supplied with coarse cloth, and the spinners, mostly women, kept making yarn. But cheaper English machine-made yarn gradually replaced homespun, and the spinners were put out of work. Cloth made in Manchester was soon found to be cheaper than cloth made locally with English yarn, and most of the weavers lost their jobs too.

Cotton spinning gave women a degree of economic independence, or at least a certain status as income earners. This was lost after the collapse of the spinning industry. The weavers of Noakhali also lost a great deal: thrown onto the land, they were left to make what they could from the sale of their crops. Buchanan's remarks on the small size of holdings in Noakhali suggest that they wouldn't have been able to pay their rent without their income from weaving. They might well have been among those who moved out to settle the new chars on the coast: for the early years of settlement, at least, rents on the chars were lower than anywhere else.

In the 1860s, after the American civil war interrupted the supply of cotton from the slave plantations, British manufacturers turned to India for their raw materials. The collector of Noakhali—the chief district officer, so called because his main job was collecting the revenue—was asked whether cotton could be grown in the district. He answered that the crop had once been widely cultivated, but wasn't any longer. 'There is no market for it', he explained. 'Formerly there were factories [trading stations] here, but our home manufactures have ousted the native produce from the market by underselling.' The exchange tells the story of the textile manufacture under imperial rule. Noakhali had once been a centre of rural industry: it was now nothing more than a possible supplier of raw materials to its former competitor. By 1876 all that remained of the manufacture were the ruins of the Company's abandoned trading stations.

CR

The textile manufacture wasn't the only rural industry to disappear from Noakhali in the course of the nineteenth century. The district had been a centre of salt production since Mughal times: in the seventeenth century a large part of Bengal's supply came from the island of Sandwip. Under the British the manufacture was a government monopoly. The salt-producing strip of land along the coast of Bengal was divided into agencies, each with a European supervisor. At the beginning of the season the supervisor gave advances to local contractors, who hired labourers to start on the work. The prices at which the salt would be sold to the supervisor, and then to the wholesale dealers, were set by the administration.

The high price of salt under the monopoly encouraged smuggling and illicit manufacture. The government responded by posting preventive officers at stations along the coast. Moheshkhali, off the coast of Chittagong, had both a salt works and a preventive station. When Francis Buchanan visited in 1798 he was told by the people living there that although salt water from the incoming tide did great damage to their crops, they couldn't afford embankments. Nor, ironically, could they afford salt. 'In the evening, I observed the poor people making Salt by soaking straw in sea water and then burning it. I am told, that Salt properly made, on account of the monopoly, is an Article much too expensive to enter into the diet of the lower Classes of people in Chittigong.'

The consumption of salt—a physiological necessity—didn't vary much from person to person. The salt tax was therefore a highly unequal one, 'heavy to the poor, imperceptible to the wealthy'. But it was the only tax that could reach all of the empire's subjects: the agricultural labourer, the boatman, the domestic worker. The government tried to justify the high level of the tax by vague references to 'the general welfare': the salt revenue was said to be 'indispensable for the preservation of peace, and for the good government of British India'. A select committee on East India finance perhaps put it more honestly when it stated that the revenue was simply 'too large to be given up'. This was especially true in Bengal, where the government had fixed the land revenue in the Permanent Settlement of 1793 and was in desperate need of alternative sources of income.

The salt department was notorious for the exploitation of its workers. There were reports in the late eighteenth century of labourers being forced to take advances for salt production, and then being sent down to the coast to be worked 'like slaves'. In 1811 the manufacture was introduced to the small island of Manpura, off the coast of Dakhin Shahbazpur: it proved so intolerable that by 1818, 350 households had been deserted. The magistrate of Bakarganj was still complaining in 1826 that the salt officers were committing 'atrocities and oppressions of every description' and using 'the greatest coercion' to get the workers to accept advances. But nothing was done to hold the department to account: the manufacture was too important to the government's finances to be interfered with.

One supervisor described the exhausting routine of labourers on the salt works at Chittagong. 'They work continually from dawn till 9:00 p.m. ... by the end of the season they are completely worn out, and could not be induced to work any longer, indeed would not be capable of doing so if it were required of them.' Three hundred salt-makers were killed by tigers in a single season in Roymangal agency, which covered Bakarganj and the district to its west, Jessore; tigers also roamed the uncultivated lands around the salt works in Noakhali. Floods and storms were a further hazard. The salt-makers were often exposed to bad weather, and after cyclones and storm-waves suffered 'a most fearful mortality'—if not from the storm itself, then from the epidemic that usually followed.

The department shrugged off criticisms of its treatment of the salt-makers. Its stock response, once it had given up coercion as a means of employment, was that they were free to leave the job if they wanted to. Henry Parker, secretary to the Board of Customs, Salt and Opium, explained rather smugly that a worker 'may be ill clothed, ill fed, and ill paid, but it still rests entirely with himself to weigh the advantages of his employment, and decide accordingly'. As for the dangers of the work, a salt-maker could expect 'no special exemption from the law of chances'. Parker was writing from the safety of his Calcutta office; he perhaps hadn't considered his own chances of being worked to death, killed by a tiger, or drowned by a storm-wave.

Revenue officials in the districts along the coast looked with longing at the great stretches of land taken up by the salt department. The salt manufacture, one wrote, was 'a great obstacle to the clearing and colonising of the chars and islands in Bakarganj and Noakhali'. There were frequent disputes on the Bakarganj side of the estuary between the holders of jungle-clearing leases and the salt officers, who wanted the forest to be preserved as a fuel supply for the salt works. (Bengal salt was made by boiling concentrated brine, rather than solar evaporation.) Yet just as it did in matters of justice, the salt department held a privileged position in matters of land, and for the time being managed to keep control of the seaboard.

The department might have been able to hold off the local magistrates and collectors, but it couldn't withstand the pressure of British commercial interests. In the 1830s British manufacturers started lobbying the Company to give up its monopoly. An 1832 select committee on the Company's affairs recommended that the industry in Bengal be scaled back and the shortfall met by salt from abroad. A few years later large quantities of British salt started coming into the province. The production costs of Bengal salt were driven up by the costs of the monopoly, and it struggled to compete with the cheaper British product. By 1851 half of the salt being consumed in Bengal had been made elsewhere. The Company was now ready to end the manufacture and restrict itself to collecting the tax on imports.

The salt industry was thought to employ about 20,000 people in Noakhali. One official, during the debate over its abolition, raised the spectre of mass unemployment and impoverishment—if only out of concern for the land revenue. 'Is it not a subject of serious inquiry whether the circulation of some lacs of rupees [a lakh was Rs. 100,000] of salt advances within a district yielding an important amount of land revenue can be withheld without imposing a degree of poverty on the inhabitants, and a consequent decrease of the revenue?' But the revenue officials had already convinced the government that its income would increase: there would now be money from newly-cultivated chars as well as from the duty on imported salt. The point about the livelihood of the workers was passed over. 'They are quite able to take care of themselves, and may well be left to do so.'

Some of the salt-makers became full-time cultivators after the manufacture ended. Others turned to cattle-keeping, taking herds out to pasture on chars that had once been covered by the barrows of the salt works. These were the lucky ones. A select committee in 1871 heard that many of the salt-makers had suffered badly after losing their jobs. 'A considerable number of them were swept from the face of the earth', the committee was told. 'They had nothing to fall back upon.'

The collapse of the salt industry brought about a major change in the pattern of land use along the coast. Chars that had been reserved for the salt department were given over to paddy cultivation and homesteads. By 1876 Beveridge thought that even if the manufacture was taken up again ('it appears strange that a country so naturally rich in salt ... should have to depend on Europe for a supply of this necessity') the chars were so highly cultivated that there wouldn't be enough jungle left for a fuel supply. Salt grounds had always been cultivated when they became higher and less saline, but this wholesale replacement was something new. More people were living along the coast than when the chars had been uninhabited fuel lands or sparsely-populated salt works; more people were exposed to the storm-waves of the Bay of Bengal.

The illicit manufacture and sale of salt became much easier to detect after the industry was abolished. The preventive officers seemed to have a presence everywhere, patrolling the Meghna for smugglers, searching the banks of creeks for signs that scrapings of saline earth had been taken, dropping in on the markets to check that no duty-free salt was being offered for sale. The landlords faced harsh penalties if their tenants were caught making salt, and came down strongly too: in 1857 a preventive officer noted approvingly that the zamindars of Dakhin Shahbazpur had become 'very strict' with their tenants 'when even the most petty salt-scraping occurs'.

The Board of Revenue admitted that the price of salt was still 'so high as greatly to restrict the use of the article, if not to place it altogether out of the reach of the poorer classes'. The question was the same as it had been earlier: 'Is the disadvantage of living where the price of Salt is so high, overbalanced by the advantage of living under a settled Government?' In 1871 the salt tax was three and a quarter rupees per maund (a weight of around 80 pounds). The price of imported salt was about half a rupee per maund. It was a tax of 650 per cent on a necessity of life.

'Do you think that the fiscal history of any civilised country in the world would furnish an example of a duty such as that?' a former lieutenant governor of Bengal was asked at a select committee hearing. 'I cannot say', he replied diplomatically. But he was less evasive—and more imperial—when asked whether the salt tax had any harmful effect on the people. 'I think the fact that they are able to bear it shows that they must be in a prosperous condition.'

CR

Revenue collection had been an obsession for the British in Bengal since 1765, when the East India Company secured the right to impose taxes on the province. The extraordinarily high tax on salt was one aspect of this obsession. Another was the number and complexity of the Company's schemes for the taxation of land. Just as it had been for the Mughals, the land tax was the Company's most important source of revenue. After several failed attempts to lease out the collection of the tax, in 1793 it entered into the Permanent Settlement with the zamindars of Bengal. This fixed the government's revenue demand once and for all at a figure equivalent to 90 per cent of the zamindars' income at the time of settlement. The zamindars were established as the absolute proprietors of the land, safe in the knowledge that they could keep any profits they might make. But if they failed to pay the revenue by sunset on the appointed day, no excuses would be accepted: their estates would be confiscated and sold at auction.

For a while the settlement seemed to work as intended. The Company received a steady income without the bother of frequent resettlements, and those zamindars who survived the early flurry of 'sunset sales' did well out of rising land values. But gradually the Company came to believe that it had sacrificed too much for too little. Few zamindars had taken advantage of the fixed tax to invest in their estates: most preferred to live on the ever-increasing rents they could demand as the population grew and land became scarcer. At the same time the Company needed higher revenues to finance its military campaigns. Giving up the right to increase the land tax now seemed to have been a mistake.

In 1814 the Company's Court of Directors observed that large areas of land in Bengal lay beyond the boundaries of the permanently settled estates, and might be made to yield a useful revenue. In 1819 the government announced its intention to bring this land under its control through 'resumption'. The tax from resumed land would give an immediate boost to the revenue, and if the settlement was made on a temporary basis it could later be increased ('enhanced') as the government required.

One of the targets for resumption was the alluvial land that had formed along the edges of the zamindars' estates since the Permanent Settlement. In 1819 the government took possession of several chars in Noakhali near the mouth of the Feni river. At the same time resumption proceedings were begun in Bakarganj: the collector travelled as far south as char Kukri Mukri, the last of the islands before the open sea, to gather information about land created since 1793. At this stage the chars around Hatia and Sandwip, and those being given up by the salt department, hadn't been properly surveyed and couldn't yet be claimed. But by the end of the 1830s nearly all the resumption suits in the estuary had been successfully completed.

In 1825 legislation was introduced to determine the rights of claimants to newly-formed alluvial lands. Under the Bengal Alluvion and Diluvion Regulation a char that formed alongside an existing tenure belonged to the holder of that tenure, subject to the payment of an additional tax. A char that formed as an island in the bed of a river or in the sea belonged to the government. Resumption could be carried out by taxing accretions to existing estates, or by taking possession of separate formations.

Both kinds of new land could be—and were—taxed at a much higher rate than land under the Permanent Settlement.

The resumption laws had serious implications for landowners in the estuary. To a surveyor a bank eroded by the river seemed to re-form very quickly indeed. But a landowner had no assurance that it would form again on the same estate. It was more likely that the eroded land would become government property: chars emerged most often as islands, only becoming part of the mainland as they expanded. If the bank did re-form on the same estate it would take several years' work by the river and the cultivators to make it productive. The zamindar might be broke and sold up before he received any rent. And even if he succeeded, the char would be resumed by the government and taxed at a higher rate than before.

The changing ownership of Sandwip estate showed how the resumption laws could be used against the zamindars. In some parts of the estate the land was being eroded by the tides, while in other parts new chars were rapidly forming. The new lands were claimed by the government. The zamindar couldn't pay the revenue demand from the land that remained, and in 1829 the government took over. By the 1860s Bamni, an island belonging to the estate, had grown so much that it had become part of the mainland; and the accretions were being taxed at rates five to twenty times higher than those of the Permanent Settlement.

A similar pattern of gains and losses could be seen on Dakhin Shahbazpur. Here the Meghna was cutting through the island's eastern bank, carrying the soil downstream and depositing it in the south. By 1876 only a small part of Dakhin Shahbazpur belonged to the estate of that name. Most of the south of the island had been resumed by the government, which with 133 chars in Bakarganj was now one of the biggest landowners in the district.

Henry Beveridge had five years' experience as collector of Bakarganj. The government's acquisition of so much land, he thought, was 'a natural consequence of the fact that the district is an alluvial formation'. But the changes in land ownership were not determined by nature. The government had turned the geography of the estuary to its own advantage, using the processes of erosion and deposition to increase its land revenue. Whatever bank their current might set against, the rivers flowed along a gradient of superior power.

The resumption of the chars brought in handsome profits. In 1795, after the Permanent Settlement had been finalised, Noakhali had paid a land revenue of Rs. 395,000. By 1871 that figure had risen to Rs. 642,000. Nearly all of the increase had come from highly taxed, temporarily settled alluvial land.

The acquisition of this new land also helped project imperial authority into the estuary. Middlemen were removed, surveys were carried out, and the local administration was tightened up. The government's increasing control over the estuary could even be seen in the names given to the new chars. Among those commemorated were British military heroes, political leaders, royalty, and ordinary district officials: Falcon, Drummond, Price, Hankey, Lord Hardinge, Lawrence, Princess Alexandra, King Sahib, Saint George, Albert, and of course Victoria.

It was fitting that so many of the chars should have been given British names. By taking possession of the new land the government had consolidated its authority and increased its land revenue. It had also developed an interest in getting people to settle that land. More cultivators meant more revenue. But it also meant more people at risk of disaster; and higher taxes left them fewer ways of avoiding that risk.

CR

A person's exposure to disaster could usually be predicted by their social position. Among the least likely to be swept away by a storm-wave were the zamindars of Noakhali. Many had never before set foot on their estates: they were absentees of the highest order, spending their lives and rental incomes in Calcutta, avoiding even the customary annual tour of their properties. The management of the land they left to underpaid agents who supplemented their wages with whatever they could extort from the tenants. The zamindars knew and cared little about what went on in the countryside: as long as they received their share of the rental income they were happy. Their properties, one collector wrote, they saw only as 'so many milch cows with whose productiveness their interest ceases'.

Noakhali had a reputation for ill health. 'The district is not famous for its salubrity,' one official wrote, 'and it is a well-known fact that no one is willing to come here, either European or native, who can keep away.' The chars that fringed the estuary were thought to be an especially potent source of disease. 'A vast expanse of steamy and offensive mud', the surveyor James Gastrell called them, 'the effluvia from which in the day-time ... is often most disgusting and oppressive.' Fever was endemic among those living nearby; Gastrell thought it was probably caused by 'miasmatic exhalations' given off by the chars and blown inland by the sea breezes.

The district also had a name for religious impurity. Wandering in exile, the Pandava brothers of the Mahabharata stopped on the right bank of the Meghna and sent Bhima across to explore the other side. Bhima reported unfavourably on the experience; the brothers left and never returned. Even in the nineteenth century a Hindu living on the Noakhali side of the Meghna was considered to be of inferior status to one of the same caste living on the Bakarganj side. An even greater stigma attached to the Hindus of Sandwip, whose standing had fallen badly during the seventeenth-century reign of the bandit chief Dilal Khan. Khan thought that marriage within caste groups produced a degenerate population: he had forced his subjects to marry across lines of caste and even religion, and the pollution had been passed down.

Little wonder that the large landowners, all of whom were high-caste Hindus or Europeans, preferred to stay in Calcutta. Civil servants thought of Bakarganj and Noakhali as hardship postings, but didn't have to leave the district headquarters very often. Lower officials couldn't escape the mofussil—the back-blocks—so easily. Dakhin Shahbazpur was the only island sub-division along the coast: the hardest of hardship postings. 'The very name of Dakhin Shahbazpur is dreaded by mostly every officer', a deputy collector stationed on the island wrote. Europeans found the 'vitiated and uncongenial climate' and the isolation from others of their kind especially trying. Indian sub-ordinates, to whom such low-ranking jobs usually fell, apparently found their situation just as distressing. 'If a native officer be asked his reasons for disliking the place, he will, after describing the big dangerous river, emphatically sum them up by saying *nona jal* [salt water] and *nona howa* [salt air].'

Such views were shared by the cultivators themselves. Rural society was divided between mainlanders and the inhabitants of the islands and chars. People knew that it was dangerous to cross over to the islands, and even more dangerous to settle on them. Parents on the mainland were reluctant to marry their daughters to char-dwellers. The more prosperous cultivators stayed well away from the coast.

Those who lived along the edges of the estuary also occupied the lowest rungs of society. After the salt-makers had disap-peared, the first to move onto the new chars were the herds-men—'a wild class of men', according to one official, and a very poor class too. The herdsmen came with their cattle at the end of the rains. They stayed until the grass dried off and the fresh water ran out. Their tenancy coincided with the worst storms of the year. Unlike later settlers, they were without even the most basic defences against the weather: they camped out on the chars in tents.

An expanding char would soon become ready for cultivation. The labour needed to prepare the land was mobilised by a developer, 'a man of energy or capital' who held a lease from the char's owner. Men from the islands or mainland were brought out to clear the scrub, plough the soil, and transplant the paddy. Most then returned to their homes; a few stayed behind in temporary shelters to watch over the crop. In November or December the crop was harvested and sold to the grain dealers who descended on the district at harvest-time.

As the height and fertility of the land increased, the developer started looking for cultivators to move to the char permanently. Colonising a char was harder work than migratory cultivation. The settlers had to build their homesteads and the paths to connect them; they had to dig and embank tanks for drinking water, excavate drainage channels, and plant groves of trees. The groves were planted with coconut and betel nut, mango, plantain, jackfruit, and silk-cotton. The trees took years to grow. Inland, on the older ground, they provided a breakwater and a refuge during floods. Aside from a few plantains bending in the breeze, the new land was bare: the homesteads, on their low earthen plinths, stood open to the sea.

CR

The decision to move to the chars was made at a time of increasing population pressure. There had been two great disasters in Bengal in the eighteenth century: the famine of 1770, which was worst in the western districts, and the flood and famine of 1787, which mainly affected the east. Since then the population had grown steadily. In the middle of the nineteenth century the rivers in the west had begun to decay, and outbreaks of epidemic malaria put an end to growth in that part of the delta. But numbers in the east continued to rise. Not only were there more people, but with the decline of the rural industries there was also greater demand for land.

The Noakhali settlement officer, reckoning backwards from the figures in the 1872 census, put the population of the mainland in 1800 at about 270,000. The population of the islands might have been as low as 20,000 (this was not including Dakhin Shahbazpur, which was transferred to Bakarganj before the census began). There was enough room for cultivation to expand without moving into the most dangerous and least productive parts of the district. In 1798 Francis Buchanan reported that in the south of Noakhali, between Lakhipur and Sudharam, 'the intervals between the plantations are much greater [than further north], and many places are in a state of nature'; Robert Knox, in 1803, wrote that most of the islands and chars in the estuary were either thinly inhabited or not inhabited at all.

By 1872 the mainland population of Noakhali had reached 687,000, and the island population 141,000. The growing population was welcomed by landlords and the government. More tenants meant more land brought under cultivation; more land meant more rent for the zamindar and his middlemen; and more rent, on land not covered by the Permanent Settlement, meant more revenue for the government. By 1876 all of the district's arable land was under cultivation: the only opportunities to take up new holdings were those opened up along the moving frontier of the chars.

The chars held out the promise of lower rents and better terms of tenure. Until the mid-nineteenth century a shortage of labour meant that settlers could often negotiate favourable rates, and for the first few years might not have to pay any rent at all. The rents of chars in the estuary were especially low because their soil, unlike that of the prodigiously fertile chars upriver, was usually sandy and salty. In the early nineteenth century Knox observed that many of the chars 'had not the most fertile appearance'; Henry Beveridge wrote that the salt efflorescence in Dakhin Shahbazpur was 'sufficient to make the soil quite white, as if covered by hoarfrost'. The risk of crops—or lives—being destroyed by floods also had a bearing on rents: on Bamni, for instance, rates were lower than elsewhere because of the frequency of salt-water flooding.

Another reason for migration was displacement by the estuary's ever-shifting rivers. At all times some part of the coast was under siege. 'There is something very desolate in the appearance of the country near these large rivers', Beveridge wrote. 'The peasants make haste to remove their houses and to cut down their groves of betel and coconut trees; as the diluvation advances, nothing is to be seen near the banks but stumps of trees, the earthen foundations of houses, and the broken walls of tanks.' Families driven away by the rivers could sometimes move inland, but more often they were pushed out onto the chars. It was a move that often meant ruin: in the local idiom they were known as the *nadi-bhanga lok*—the river-broken people.

In his novel *Padma River Boatman* the Bengali writer Manik Bandyopadhyay tells the story of Kuber, a Hindu fisherman and boatman, and his eventual migration to one of the chars. The boatmen of Kuber's village are patronised by Hossain Mian, a Muslim trader and land developer. Mian has bought a small island off the Noakhali mainland called Moynadwip. He has already taken three families from the village, in debt and facing starvation, to the island. Kuber and the other boatmen are afraid of him. He is charismatic and persuasive, and seems to sympathise with their difficulties. But he also has a reputation for inflicting terrible punishments on anyone who gets in his way. To the boatmen his will seems like a force beyond nature: 'Whatever he brought about happened in its course and was inevitable.'

One day Rasu, a boatman who has been living on Moynadwip, returns to the village. He is broken by the labour of clearing and cultivating the island; his wife and children are dead. Mian has to pacify the angry villagers. 'Which fellow did I take to Moynadwip forcibly? You had gone of your own accord; if you're honest you must admit it.' (The salt department had used the same argument against the hapless salt-makers: that everybody had the same choices about where to live and what work to do.)

Presently there is a storm on the Padma, the tail end of a cyclone. Kuber, needing the money, has gone out on the river in the knowledge that bad weather is on its way. He has a narrow escape, and when he gets back finds that his hut has been damaged. Mian supplies him with the materials to repair it. Then he offers him a job in one of his boats. Kuber knows that 'any favour accepted from Hossain Mian will ultimately do no good'. But the fishing season on the Padma is coming to an end, and without a boat of his own he can't find any other work, so he agrees.

For some time Mian has been trying to persuade another boatman, Aminuddi, to go down to Moynadwip. Finally, after his wife is killed in the storm, Aminuddi gives in. 'They felt it was not the storm, but Hossain Mian who had destroyed Aminuddi's hut by felling the mango tree over it. It was said that some people control ghosts and spirits; goodness knows whether Hossain Mian had similar powers too!'

Kuber sets out for the estuary with Aminuddi and a poor Muslim family recruited from another village. Moynadwip is so low 'that it would seem as if the sea might swallow it up any day it wished'. Its centre is a salty swamp, but other parts are producing good harvests. The work of clearance and cultivation is back-breaking; life on the island is 'ruthless and silent'. Of the hundred or so inhabitants about a third are small children, most of them born there. Mian keeps a keen eye on the growth of the population: people, to him, are profit. He has Aminuddi married to one of the women of the Muslim family as soon as possible. 'People like Aminuddi who were left battered, disheartened and demoralised in the battles of life were not actually needed by him; the generation of boys and girls they would populate his island with were the ones he was waiting for.'

Kuber goes back to his village, but isn't there for long. He is framed for a theft by Rasu, the former settler. Rasu is angry at him for giving his daughter to a man of Hossain Mian's choosing—a man who, of course, is also destined for the colony. Kuber can't afford to pay off the police, and flees to Mian's house to avoid arrest. Mian offers to take him to Moynadwip; his family will be sent after him. Kuber knows well enough the life that awaits him there, but is in no position to refuse. Once again Hossain Mian has got what he wanted. The story, though, has proposed that his power over the boatmen is derived not from the supernatural, but from his wealth and their wretchedness.

CR

James Rennell's description of a flood that swept over Lakhipur in 1763 is perhaps the only eighteenth-century record of a storm-wave in the Meghna estuary. 'A very tragical event happened ... by a strong gale of wind conspiring with a high spring tide, at a season when the periodical flood was within a foot and a half of its highest pitch. It is said that the rivers rose 6 feet above the ordinary level ... it happened in a part of the country which scarce provides a tree for a drowning man to escape to.' Rennell was writing before the storm-wave had become a recognised phenomenon, but his description suggests something more destructive than just a high tide and gale.

There had already been several catastrophic storm-waves in Noakhali and Bakarganj in the nineteenth century: in 1822, 1825, 1848, and again in 1867. Only a strong sea-wall could have stood against them. Yet none of the chars had such a wall, or even an embankment capable of keeping out an unusually high tide. Most were entirely unprotected. Two chars to the south of Sudharam, Darvesh and Jagadananda, had been partly embanked, but their works counted for little in a cyclone. The storm-wave of 1867 broke the embankments, flooded the crops with salt water, and washed away the cultivators' homesteads and cattle. The situation was similar on the embanked estate of Nilakhi, on Hatia: here the wave of 1867 spoilt a quarter of the paddy, though the damage was less serious than it would have been without protective works. The only other notable embankment in the estuary was on Siddhi, just north of Sandwip. Everywhere else the inhabitants of the chars were totally exposed to the sea.

The building of large embankments demanded resources beyond those of the cultivators or even their landlords. Traditionally the responsibility had belonged to the state. Yet in the hundred or so years that the British government had collected Noakhali's taxes, it had financed only the manifestly inadequate embankments on char Darvesh.

The cultivators knew the danger they were in, and so did the district administration. In May 1869 Bamni, on the Noakhali coast, was flooded by salt water for the fourth time in five years. The superintendent of police visited afterwards. 'The people expressed anxiety on the subject of an embankment', he reported. 'They naturally wish to be secure, and are willing to pay half the costs if an embankment is granted.'

The offer was ignored: no embankment would be built on Bamni, or in any other part of the estuary. Just a few months before the 1876 cyclone the collector of Noakhali, Reginald Porch, described the idea of building protective works along the Meghna as 'absurd'. Any such structures, he said, would be reduced to rubble by the first high spring tide. The practical problem could perhaps be solved by placing the embankments a mile or two inland, leaving the stretch between river and wall to absorb the force of the wave. But the financial question remained. On this point Porch was clear. 'It does not appear ... to be worthwhile to go to the enormous expense of constructing a system of embankments merely to avoid a loss of crops occurring so rarely.'

The lives at risk do not seem to have entered Porch's calculations. As recently as 1864 a storm-wave on the western seaboard had drowned around 50,000 people. A similar number had died in Bakarganj and Noakhali in the cyclone of 1822. There was also the disruption to the livelihoods of the survivors, the hunger, the outbreaks of disease: all subsumed, in Porch's accounting, under 'a loss of crops'.

When it came to making hard decisions, the prosperity and security of the empire's subjects—the 'moral and material progress' recounted in the annual administration reports—took second place to profits. The opportunities of the new frontier had gone to those with the power and money to take advantage of them: the government, the landlords, the contractors and leaseholders. The weavers and salt-makers who had been put out of work—along with the boatmen, herdsmen, labourers, and cultivators—were the ones who had to live with its risks.

2

THE FOREST

In the eighteenth century the mangrove forest of the Sundarbans grew deep and thick along the coast of Bengal, from the Meghna estuary in the east to the Hooghly in the west. 'That part of the delta bordering on the sea', James Rennell reported, 'is composed of a labyrinth of rivers and creeks ... so completely enveloped in woods, and infested with tygers, that if any attempts have ever been made to clear it (as is reported) they have hitherto miscarried.'

Now it was time for another attempt. 'If these tracts were contiguous to England,' one traveller wrote, 'how soon the desert wild would be cleared by enterprise and industry, and the tigers driven from their haunts!'

British attitudes towards the Sundarbans were shaped by an idea of 'improvement'. The idea had moral as well as agricultural implications. In a tract written in 1792, the politician and evangelist Charles Grant described India as 'a country peculiarly calculated by its natural advantages, to promote the happiness of its inhabitants'. The people of India, though, were 'a race of men lamentably degenerate and base, sunk in misery by their vices'.

Grant thought that Indian morals would be most surely improved through the propagation of Christianity. But he also thought that advances in agriculture would play a part. A cultivator who was 'far more likely to die from want, than to relieve himself by any new or extraordinary effort', was fortunate now to be in the hands of a people 'skilled to make the most of soils and seasons, to improve the existing modes of culture, of pasturage, of rearing cattle, of defence against excess of drought, and of rain'.

Improvement demanded that land and labour be controlled by whoever could make the most efficient use of them. This was the principle behind the Permanent Settlement of 1793, which gave the tax-collecting zamindars of Bengal absolute rights of private property in land (and turned the tax-paying cultivators into tenants). It was Lord Cornwallis who introduced the settlement during his first term as governor general. Cornwallis was a member of the English landed gentry, and his sympathies were with their nearest Bengali equivalents. His hope was that the zamindars would become improving landlords of the familiar English variety. Subject only to a moderate, fixed tax, they would put their capital towards 'purchasing and improving lands': clearing forest, draining marshes, building embankments and tanks.

The zamindars never became the agents of improvement Cornwallis had hoped for. But enthusiasm for the idea remained. Its most important spokesman in Bengal was the Baptist missionary William Carey, who founded the Agricultural and Horticultural Society of India in 1820. The Society's aim was 'the cultivation of large tracts of country, now not only useless, but the resort of savage beasts, and the source of severe diseases'; it also looked to 'the gradual conquest of that indolence, which in Asiatics is almost become a second nature, and the introduction ... of industry and virtue in the room of idleness and vice'.

It was confident vision. But the land and people that were to be transformed were only half understood; and the vision would not survive the disappointments and disasters that were to come.

CR

Improvement could make cutting down the forest seem like an imperial obligation. There was also money to be made, though, and here duty became indistinguishable from the Company's attempts to increase its land revenue.

The Company had inherited the land revenue system of Murshid Quli Khan, the powerful finance minister who became governor of Bengal in 1717. Murshid Quli's innovation had been to contract a group of middlemen—the future zamindars of Bengal—to collect the revenue from the cultivators and pay it into the treasury. In 1722 he made the first new assessment of the land revenue in 140 years. The demand was Rs. 14,000,000: a high figure at the time. Later rulers asked for more. By 1756 the demand had risen to Rs. 19,000,000; and in 1760, under the beleaguered governor Mir Qasim, it reached Rs. 24,000,000.

The Company's revenue demands were even higher than Mir Qasim's. It needed the money to pay its large army and rapidly expanding bureaucracy; it also needed to finance its 'investment'—its system of extracting wealth from Bengal by using locally raised taxes to buy goods for export. After 1772 the Company took direct responsibility for collecting the province's taxes. Its assessments ranged from Rs. 25,000,000 to Rs. 28,000,000. The Permanent Settlement was fixed at Rs. 27,000,000. Mir Qasim's actual collections had been much lower than his demands. The Company was better organised, and managed to bring in virtually the full amount of its assessments.

The Company soon developed an interest in the Sundarbans as a potential source of land revenue, and in 1770 began granting leases to cut down the forest and replace it with tax-paying cultivation. In 1783 Tilman Henckell, the magistrate of Jessore,

sent the Board of Revenue his plan for the 'wholesale reclamation' of the forest. Henckell proposed to open up the Sundarbans
by giving out generous grants to prospective developers. The
grants would be tax-free for the first three years; after that a low
tax, rising to the full rate by the seventh year, would be applied
to land brought under cultivation. His plan, he explained, would
turn land that was otherwise 'totally unproductive' into a source
of profit. He expected that 200,000 acres of forest would be
taken in grants, and that in the first seven years those grants
would produce a revenue of Rs. 750,000.

The Board approved the plan, and Henckell was appointed
'Superintendent for Cultivating the Sundarbans'. But there was
a complication. The zamindars along the forest's northern border
said that their estates ran to the Bay of Bengal in the south, and
that the land Henckell had been giving out actually belonged to
them. To support their claims they sent out small teams of cultivators to clear patches of forest in the south. They also sent out
armed retainers to sabotage the first attempts at cultivation on
the grants. The developers fell behind on their payments, and the
profits Henckell had so confidently predicted never arrived.
Henckell thought that if the question of ownership was decided
he could still succeed. But the Board didn't want to get involved
in an expensive court case against the zamindars, and in 1790
withdrew its support for the scheme.

For the next twenty-five years the Sundarbans was forgotten
by the revenue administrators, focused as they were on the work-
ings of the Permanent Settlement. But the same pressures that
had prompted the resumption of alluvial land in the estuary—
the fixed land revenue and the costs of military expansion—eventually directed their attention towards the forest. In 1814 the
Board of Revenue took up the question of the Sundarbans again.
The forest, it declared, belonged to the state, not to the zamindars. It followed that the government was entitled to a revenue

from all Sundarbans land that had been brought into cultivation since the Permanent Settlement, and that it could dispose of the rest of the forest however it pleased.

The Company's surveyors soon moved into the Sundarbans, measuring the land that had been cleared since the Permanent Settlement and the great stretches of forest that remained. The appointment of a Sundarbans commissioner in 1816 brought the area under a single revenue jurisdiction. Regulations passed in 1817 and 1819 established the government's right to resume cultivated land that lay beyond the boundaries of the zamindars' estates. And the debate over who owned the remaining forest was settled emphatically by Regulation III of 1828: 'the uninhabited tract known by the name of the Sundarbans has ever been, and is hereby declared still to be, the property of the State'.

William Dampier, the Sundarbans commissioner, arrived in Bakarganj in 1830. He found that clearances had been made 'most extensively' since the Permanent Settlement. The rate of clearance had been especially high in the last twenty years. Half of the Rabnabad islands had been deforested, and large numbers of Maghs, immigrants from the Arakan coast, had occupied clearings along the southern edge of the mainland. Dampier set about assessing this recently cleared land for tax. He worked thoroughly and conceded little to the zamindars; he even managed to resume some land, such as the island of Manpura, that had clearly belonged to an established estate at the time of the Permanent Settlement. And his proceedings were highly successful: 85,000 acres of cultivated land in the Sundarbans were resumed, and nearly Rs. 100,000 was added to the revenue.

The clearances Dampier found in Bakarganj could be partly explained by the pressures of the Permanent Settlement. In the years immediately after the settlement the largest estates in Bengal had been sold at auction for arrears of revenue. Scheming subordinates, interfering officials, family feuds, calamities, debt, and simple incompetence had all contributed to their collapse. Often most important, though, was the proportion of tax to agricultural resources. In theory the revenue demand was fixed at 90 per cent of the zamindar's rental income at the time of settlement. But the actual figure depended on the accuracy of the information gathered beforehand. This in turn depended on the size of the estate (large estates were investigated more thoroughly than smaller ones) and its level of cultivation (well-developed estates were investigated more thoroughly than 'backward' ones). The zamindars of large, highly cultivated estates in Bakarganj were taxed heavily in 1793, and soon lost control of their properties. But the zamindars of estates bordering the Sundarbans managed to survive. They still had patches of jungle on their estates, and could increase their rental income by bringing in new tenants to clear and cultivate the land. Until 1830, when they lost this source of income to Dampier and his resumption proceedings, they could also arrange for parts of the forest itself to be cleared.

Resumed Sundarbans lands were usually temporarily settled. Instead of the land tax being fixed forever, as it had been on land assessed in 1793, it was set for a short time, often twenty years. After this it could be increased as the government required. Even if the rate wasn't increased, the starting rates for temporary settlements were much higher than those of the Permanent Settlement. Without having to offer any concessions for the clearance of these once-forested lands, the government had managed to turn them into a useful source of revenue.

ॐ

The resumption of existing cultivation was only one of the government's sources of Sundarbans revenue. Now that the ownership of the forest had been clearly established, it could be opened up to a new generation of prospective improvers. In 1830 a system of government grants was introduced that took up where Henckell's plan had left off, but on even easier terms: twenty years tax-free, the full rate to be paid after twenty-four.

Applications soon started coming into the commissioner's office, mostly from Europeans in Calcutta expecting to make big profits under such generous terms. But again the scheme was less successful in practice than on paper. Many of the developers, especially in the western and central Sundarbans, failed to meet the condition that they clear a quarter of their block within five years. Some had only been buying speculatively and had no immediate plans to cut down the forest. Others, especially those with grants in the south-west, found it hard to attract tenants: a lack of fresh water and the risk of flooding kept away all but the most desperate.

Those grant-holders who did find tenants lost many of them to cyclones and storm-waves—in 1833, 1842, and 1848. Yet the government was reluctant to give up the scheme, and carried on as if nothing had happened. The only challenge to its studied avoidance of the problem came from Henry Piddington, a former commander in the merchant marine. Piddington had been interested in the storms of the Bay of Bengal for several years. (In 1848 he had proposed that the word 'cyclone'—from the Greek 'the coil of a snake'—should be used to describe them.) In 1853 there was a proposal to build a port in the Sundarbans. Piddington wrote an open letter to the governor general, Lord Dalhousie, warning him of the dangers of the plan. 'Every thing and every one must be prepared to see a day when, in the midst of the horrors of a hurricane, they will find a terrific mass of salt water rolling in ... such a visitation may not occur for the next five years, or for the next twenty years; but it may also occur in the coming month of October.'

The warning was ignored. Just a few weeks later the government further relaxed the terms of the grants. The revenue,

Dalhousie said, was now of secondary importance: the main thing was 'to effect a clearance of that pestilent jungle in the shortest possible period, and to remove the stigma which most justly attaches to the existence of such a nuisance almost within sight of the Capital'. The forest, he continued, 'spreads disease and death over the whole country ... swarms with tigers and other wild beasts, and affords convenient shelter for smugglers and river pirates'; the government was obliged to do all it could to 'remove ... this source of so much material suffering'.

There was now a note of desperation in the rhetoric of the improvers. And even under the new rules, grant-holders in the 24 Parganas (south of Calcutta) and Jessore had little success. It was becoming clear that the problem wasn't one of moral capacity, or of tax incentives, but of geography. The channels of the western delta had lost their connection to the main branch of the Ganges, and were closer to being arms of the sea than rivers. The rivers of eastern Bengal were fed by the Ganges and Brahmaputra and brought down vast amounts of fresh water, especially during the rains. The eastern rivers also brought down vast amounts of sand and silt, which built up the land; the western rivers carried so little that the land on that side of the delta was subsiding.

Salinity and subsidence made reclamation in the west much more expensive than in the east. 'To obtain any profits from grants in the western Soonderbuns,' one surveyor wrote, 'expensive embankments and sluices must be constructed. In many parts of Bakarganj it is only necessary to cut down the trees.' Cutting down the trees was hard work, and the isolation of Bakarganj caused other problems. Yet compared with the western and central Sundarbans, deforestation in Bakarganj had been a success. In the 1860s the revenue surveyor, James Gastrell, reported that since Dampier had marked out the forest boundary thirty years earlier cultivation had 'extended very much', replacing 'dense heavy forest'. There were clearings all over the district, and deforestation was going ahead rapidly. Along the banks of the Meghna the Sundarbans was cleared down to the sea. In 1872 the Sundarbans commissioner calculated that the area of forest had been reduced by half since the government introduced its system of grants in 1830: only 77 square miles in Pirozpur subdivision and 261 square miles in Patuakhali remained.

No protective works had been put up in place of the forest. The rivers and creeks of Bakarganj were fresh for most of the year, and embankments to keep salt water off the crops were usually not necessary. A few of the clearings closest to the sea had been embanked, but not very substantially. 'Were I required to report on them,' one traveller wrote, 'it would be, that they require both height and breadth to render them secure and durable.' Yet they were now, after the destruction of the forest, all that stood between the cultivators and the storm-waves of the Bay of Bengal.

◌੪

In the more saline and low-lying parts of the forest the doctrine of improvement had been defeated by stubborn physical realities. But the government still needed money, and in the 1870s the doctrine of conservation was taken up as a way of making an income from the Sundarbans that didn't depend on wholesale clearance and cultivation.

The government's conservation policy had grown out of its need to secure access to forest resources, especially timber for the railways. A forest department was established in 1864, and work began on the management of India's forests for commercial production (and the exclusion from them of their traditional users). In 1869 the new department suggested that part of the Sundarbans should be conserved. It was the first sign that the single-minded pursuit of reclamation might be coming to an end. But the timber of the Sundarbans had no apparent commercial value, and the suggestion was rejected.

In 1872 the conservator of forests in Bengal, Wilhelm Schlich, presented a plan for making an income from the Sundarbans. Great quantities of timber, firewood, and other forest produce, he explained, were being taken without adding anything to the revenue. A line of toll stations along the forest boundary, supported by a fleet of patrol boats, might bring in Rs. 150,000 a year.

The government thought that such a scheme would be more trouble than it was worth. But Schlich was determined to bring the forest under the department's control. Earlier he had described the Sundarbans as 'an inexhaustible resource'; he now said that it was in danger of being destroyed by gangs of wood-cutters. 'Even in the soonder tracts', he reported, 'one sees nothing but dead soonder trees and seedlings.' (The red-wooded *sundri*, used especially for boat-building, was the most valuable timber tree of the Sundarbans; according to some accounts the forest had been named after it.)

After touring the Sundarbans in 1874 the new lieutenant governor of Bengal, Sir Richard Temple, agreed. The remaining forest, especially the stands of sundri, had to be protected. 'Reclamation is not wanted', Temple declared. 'In some places the substitution of rice-fields for jungle may be desirable. But in this particular case the ground already bears produce which is more valuable to Bengal than rice.' In 1875 it was announced that 885 square miles of forest in Jessore would be reserved and a royalty placed on sundri timber; in 1876 another 700 square miles in Jessore and the 24 Parganas was added to the reserve.

The government had realised that exports of forest produce made an important contribution to the economy of southern Bengal, and might also make a contribution to its income. But the argument for conservation succeeded only because reclamation had already failed. Much of the forest land in the 24 Parganas and Jessore was too low-lying and saline to be profitably cultivated, and there was no reason to object to that part of the Sundarbans being reserved.

It was only after the cyclone of 1864 that officials noticed the role of the Sundarbans in protecting people from storm-waves. The storm did great damage to British shipping in the port of Calcutta, and washed away many of the inhabitants of the grants in the 24 Parganas. James Gastrell co-authored a report for the government on the event. When he arrived in Bakarganj to carry out the revenue survey he was surprised at how much forest had gone from the eastern side of the delta. 'Care should ... be taken eventually', he wrote, 'to preserve a broad belt of forest between the clearings and the bay, to protect them from the encroachment of the sea during storms.'

James Westland made a similar observation in his 1871 account of the neighbouring district of Jessore. 'Liability to cyclones must put a practical limit to the extension of cultivation, for the nearer one gets to the sea, the greater the danger; and the more the forest is cleared away, the smaller the barrier placed between the cultivator and the devouring wave.' And the point was made again in 1875 by William Wilson Hunter, who described the belt of forest along the coast as 'an admirable breakwater against the ocean'. (The most common tree in the Bakarganj Sundarbans, *keora*, grew to heights of 50 or 60 feet—well above the highest recorded storm-wave.) During the cyclone of 1869, Hunter wrote, the forest had broken the force of the storm-wave before it reached the cultivated areas 'and thus prevented a great deal of destruction of life and property'.

Official awareness of the dangers of deforestation had no effect on official policy. In Jessore and the 24 Parganas the question lost its significance after the reservation of the forest, for quite different reasons, in 1875. In Bakarganj it was simply ignored. The cultivation of the Bakarganj Sundarbans wasn't subject to the natural disadvantages of the western districts, and conservation was never seriously considered. On a few islands, Gastrell reported, the Magh cultivators had kept a belt of trees as a breakwater, 'varying in depth according to the exposure of the situation'. But this was an exception. Most of those living in the clearings along the coast and the banks of the rivers would be swept away by the next storm-wave.

☙

At the end of the rains the woodcutters of Bakarganj left their homes in the north and went down in their boats to the very south of the district. Before starting work they made a clearing at the edge of the forest and put up a small shrine to the forest deity Bon Bibi. The fakir they had brought with them made offerings and sacrifices to the deity and received the power to keep them from harm. Despite his presence, though, the wood-cutters were often carried off by tigers, and sometimes by the saltwater crocodiles that lived in the creeks. 'They are very poor and must venture their lives to gain their living', one official explained. 'Their choice lies between starvation and risking themselves against the tigers.'

The woodcutters took only the most valuable timber species. Much of the wholesale clearance of the Bakarganj Sundarbans was done by the Maghs, immigrants from the Arakan coast. The Maghs were thought to make better forest clearers than the Bengalis, and were different in other ways too from their puritanical Muslim neighbours—their leisure they spent drinking rice beer or palm liquor, tattooing themselves, gambling, playing tug of war, and smoking opium and tobacco (the women stored their half-smoked cheroots in holes bored in their ears). The Maghs disliked paying rent or revenue, and after cutting down the trees usually cultivated the land for a few years before moving on. By the 1870s, though, many were living in regular settlements on estates or government grants.

Turning the forest into cultivated fields was hard work. 'The trees intertwine with each other to such an extent', one official wrote, 'that each upholds and supports the other; and some of the trees are an immense size ... Trees like these cannot be cut down and removed in bulk; they must be taken piecemeal.' An aggressive tiger could make a group of labourers abandon land they had been working on for years. Tree stumps and roots made newly-cleared land impossible to plough; the foot-high prongs sent up by the mangroves made it nearly impossible to work on. If the land was neglected it would become an impenetrable jungle of reeds within a year.

As in the rest of Bakarganj, paddy was the most important crop in the Sundarbans. There were two types. Autumn rice was sown broadcast on higher land and harvested in September and October; winter rice was transplanted from seedbeds and harvested in December and January. In the south of the district the cultivators depended almost entirely on the winter crop. Most years great quantities of winter rice were exported from Bakarganj to the rest of Bengal. The district was famous for its balam rice, which took its name from the long, low balam boats it was transported in. Balam rice came from the centre of Bakarganj and went to Calcutta; the crop in the south, though plentiful, was coarser and went mainly to Dacca.

The success or failure of the crops in Bakarganj depended on the annual floods. The network of rivers and creeks distributed the flood waters right across the district, spreading the silt that produced the winter rice. The ideal flood began to cover the soil in June, rose until September, and then fell again at the same speed. A sudden rise when the crop was young could be disastrous, but was not common. There were also times when rainfall was important:

> If the land is dry in Jaistha and gets good rain in Ashar
> Then it cannot bear the weight of the crop.
> If there is rain without a cyclone in Kartik
> Where can the paddy be stored?

Dry heat after ploughing in the month of Jaistha (May–June) killed the weeds; rain in Ashar (June–July) helped in preparing the seedbeds. By Kartik (October–November) the waters were subsiding, and rain helped bring out the ear of the paddy. But this was also the month when the crops could be destroyed by the winds of a cyclone, or by the storm-wave accompanying it.

CR

'The few cases of poverty among the cultivating class', William Wilson Hunter wrote in his account of the Sundarbans, 'result from folly and idleness, not from misfortune or oppression.' In Bakarganj, though, exploitation by the landlords had its effects on the prosperity and security of the cultivators.

Bakarganj was infamous for its system of subdivided land tenure—'the most tortuous and intricate system of land tenure in the world', one collector called it. The system went back to the revenue hunger of the late Mughal and early British administrations. In the political chaos of the eighteenth century it had been easy for old estate boundaries to be redrawn and new leases issued. The authorities were obsessed with increasing the revenue, and generous in dispensing forest-clearing grants.

The new landlords were under pressure to bring their properties under cultivation as quickly as possible. But they were unable to organise wholesale deforestation on their own. They solved the problem by granting forest-clearing tenures-in-chief for their uncultivated lands. The holders of these tenures, usually wealthy men from Dacca, had no intention of moving to the forests of Bakarganj. So they sublet their grants to others, some of whom undertook to mobilise a band of labourers or cultivators and take them down to the forest. Others sublet again; and in the very south of the district, where leases were largest, that sub-lessee might sublet yet again. At the time of the Permanent Settlement there were already two or three grades of under-tenure beneath the original grant-holder. And the tenure chain kept growing, until by the 1870s there might be seven or eight intermediaries between the landlord and the actual cultivator.

Like their counterparts in Noakhali, the biggest landowners of nineteenth-century Bakarganj were absentees. The holders of the three largest properties were Khajah Ahsanullah of Dacca and the representatives of the Ghosal and Tagore families of Calcutta. Henry Beveridge thought that none of them had ever visited the district. Bakarganj was a long way from Dacca, and further from Calcutta; it was notorious for dacoits, or gang robbers; the salt air was bad for the health; the rivers were dangerous. The only zamindars who lived in the district were the poorer ones, and even they were absentees of a kind, usually living at Barisal, the district headquarters. Many of the superior tenure-holders lived in Dacca or Faridpur. The holders of smaller tenures in the north of the district might live on their land, but few in the formerly forested south did.

An expandable and flexible system of land tenure had its advantages in the Sundarbans, where the land had already been subdivided by the rivers and creeks. But it also increased the economic pressure on those at the bottom of the tenure chain. The first description of subdivided tenure in Bakarganj is in a letter by William Dampier, the Sundarbans commissioner; the letter was written while he was carrying out resumption proceedings in the south of the district in the early 1830s. 'I have been much struck whilst employed in this district by the general wretched condition of the lower orders. I was most particularly surprised, as I found the country itself was most fertile ... whilst large markets are situated, so as to take off all the surplus produce ... Their condition could not therefore have arisen from the want of a vent for their produce, nor from the poverty of the soil not giving a sufficient return to their labour.'

Dampier blamed the landlords—the zamindars and their middlemen—for the situation. Most of the property in an estate was made up of under-tenures: there were also small pockets where the zamindar collected rent directly from the cultivators. The tenure-holders had discovered that the money they were supposed to give as rent to the zamindar could be better used in other ways. They had set up as traders and moneylenders, and were speculating in grain and advancing money and rice to the cultivators. The advances they recovered after the harvest with 50 per cent interest. The profits were impressive: in the years between 1820 and 1831 the grant-holder of Chota Basdia, a small island estate bordering the Bay of Bengal, made Rs. 100,000.

The middlemen did so well out of their tenants that the zamindar often had to take them to court to collect his rents. In the meantime he had to borrow money to pay the government's revenue demand. He paid the interest on his loan by rack-renting the tenants in those pockets of the estate he still had access to. And that wasn't the end of it. The middlemen might finally be forced by the court to pay the interest on the zamindar's loan and his legal expenses. The money would come not from the profits of their speculation or lending, but from new taxes on their tenants or increased rents on their lands, 'to such an extent as to render subsistence on them almost a matter of impossibility'.

Dampier was uncomfortable with the situation in Bakarganj, but did little to improve it. He gave proprietary rights in most resumed estates (except the few brought under government management) to the superior tenure-holders; although they lived away from their estates, he decided that they were 'the actual occupiers'. The zamindars had played no part in the clearances and were left out of the equation. The fact of subdivided tenure was acknowledged by setting the revenue demand in proportion to the number of under-tenures, so that an estate with a higher number of tenures would pay a lower revenue to the government, and vice versa. All the intermediaries were listed on the rent roll, a record of the rates that the different grades of tenant were expected to pay (and a defence against extortion by a higher tenure-holder). The actual cultivators, who had suffered most at the hands of the middlemen, received no legal recognition at all: they were left as they had been before the resumption proceedings, 'mere labourers destitute of all rights'.

ᴄᴙ

The imperial revenue records and administrative reports make much of the attractions of jungle clearing for cultivators. Rents were low and the terms of tenure were favourable: when labour was scarce these were necessary enticements to distant and dangerous places. But little is really known about rates of rent in nineteenth-century Bengal. The zamindars and other landlords took great pains to hide their books from surveyors and district officers. The official figures that Hunter copied into his *Statistical Account of Bengal* suggest that rent demands in the Sundarbans were between 15 and 25 per cent of the total value of the produce. The figures in the landlords' books, though, would probably have been quite different.

In theory rents were set according to the fertility and location of a holding, its size, and the crops grown on it. Every estate had an elaborate table of rates, which were in turn regulated by the general rates of the revenue division. But without regular estate surveys the figures lost much of their meaning. On Dakhin Shahbazpur, for instance, the formal rates were found to be 'fictitious and imaginary'; the real rates were 'a matter of mutual contract', of 'give and take'. Every important tenant had his own special arrangement—so much the worse for those who couldn't spare a little extra for a favourable assessment.

Rents were compounded by a number of illegal taxes known as *abwab*. At the time of the Permanent Settlement all additional taxes had been bound up in the rent and the introduction of new ones forbidden. That law was disregarded by the landlords of

Bakarganj. In Patuakhali subdivision abwab were never less than a quarter of the rent, and often much more. On one of the rare occasions that a landlord's books were seen it was found that he had collected more abwab that year than rent. A charge to pay the landlord's agents was universal, and a charge on marriages among tenants widespread. Hindu landlords often added an extra charge for remarriage among their Muslim tenants, and cultivators could even be forced to pay for the extravagant marriage celebrations of the landlord's family. Abwab were also levied to set up a market, to pay for temple worship, or to build an embankment, bridge, or tank.

Abwab proliferated in the second half of the nineteenth century as zamindars increased the scope and scale of their demands instead of raising rents. Rent increases might have given higher returns, but they might also have attracted protest or government intervention. Abwab offered a more flexible and sensitive means of exploitation. Perhaps most importantly, their collection gave landlords an intoxicating sense of personal power. 'He feels that as the recipient of rent he is merely the lord of land,' the Bakarganj settlement officer James Jack wrote, 'but as the recipient of abwab he is the lord of subjects. Many landlords have confessed to me that the delight of the abwab is in the arrogation of sovereignty.' The arrogation of sovereignty: there could be no clearer statement of the empire within an empire that the zamindars of Bakarganj had carved out for themselves. On the forest frontier they ruled over their tenants like princes over their subjects.

There were times when taxes and rents could only be collected through coercion. The courts of rural Bengal—along with the police stations and collectorates—were instruments of the landlords as much as of the government. There was, one magistrate wrote, a 'formidable and well-organised system of false witnesses, false accounts, bribery and corruption'. If a tenant refused to pay an abwab the landlord could threaten to sue for arrears of rent: many landlords, especially in the south of Bakarganj, refused to give receipts for rent paid. (Others insisted that an abwab be given in exchange for a receipt.) If the courts failed, intransigent tenants could be dealt with by the landlord's private army. One estate in the south had over 400 clubmen, who were hired out to neighbouring estates that couldn't afford a standing force.

Cultivators could expect little help from the law. Regulations passed in 1799 and 1812 upheld the rights of zamindars to imprison their tenants (most estates had their own dungeon or lock-up). The tenants' own rights were deliberately left undefined. The Rent Act of 1859 was the first attempt to give the cultivators some kind of legal protection. Those who had held their lands for twelve years were given the right of continued occupancy, and rent increases were restricted to economic grounds such as the extension of cultivation or an increase in prices. The Act also removed the landlords' powers of imprisonment. The zamindars, though, were left firmly in control: tenants' cattle and other assets could still be seized, and those who hadn't occupied their land for twelve years could still be evicted at will.

The Rent Act had its strengths and weaknesses, but in the south of Bakarganj it was hardly worth the paper it was written on. The civil and criminal courts were in Barisal, a five-day journey from the coast; a group of petitioners reminded the court registrar that just getting to court involved 'crossing and recrossing a great many formidable rivers'. And the rivers were perhaps the least of the obstacles the cultivators faced. After they reached Barisal there were all sorts of legal expenses: registering a suit, bribing a minor official to get the case heard, paying for stamps, engaging a pleader. Attendance at court took them away from their homes and fields for weeks at a time, and delays in the proceedings could be expensive.

Justice, in the south of Bakarganj, was the province of the landlords and their agents. The diary kept by a zamindar during the annual cold-weather tour of his estate offers a glimpse into how this justice was dispensed:

'2nd February. From 4:10 p.m. the tenants began to come and paid nazar [a monetary gift]. Asked all of them who they suspect as the culprit of Chandra Sil's theft case. They all went to shore and when they came back they all said that they suspect Hazari Khan as the culprit ... ordered Rohimuddi to shoe-beat Hazari Khan as all the tenants suspect him to be the thief, but he does not confess his guilt ... retired for the night. God save me from all troubles in the night and bless me for the next morning so that I may realise money in abundance as miscellaneous receipt.

'4th February. Tenants came to pay nazar ... Instructed the peons and mridhas [local strongmen] how they will conduct the business here in my absence. One who will disobey me must be oppressed with iron hands, whoever he may be—this was my instruction to my men. Very pleasant. Everybody pleased.

'9th February. Imam Bux, who I believe most, said that really the tenants are in most wretched condition owning to the failure of crops ... nearly 20, 25 men came to complain against the imposition of nazar at the rate of Rs. 2 ... Sat in a chair and ordered that in consideration of the bad condition of the tenants of this village, they will pay Rs. 1 as nazar.'

Such was the landlord's progress: collecting fines, receiving salutations, giving orders, supervising punishments, and occasionally displaying a benevolence that only revealed the almost unlimited extent of his power.

Cultivators could respond to an unusually oppressive landlord or his agents simply by abandoning that estate and moving elsewhere. 'Desertions take place in large numbers', a settlement officer working in the Sundarbans reported in the 1850s. 'A flourishing property is abandoned or nearly abandoned—deterioration rapidly follows—cultivation is arrested in its progress ... and before five years can pass away, a jungle springs up where a paddy field once existed.' This strategy, though, became less effective as land became scarcer.

Cultivators who were unhappy with their landlord could also transfer their allegiance to another. In return for taking the group under his protection the new landlord would gain prestige and the right to collect abwab, leaving the original landlord with only the rent from the land. Such shifts in allegiance were the source of many violent disputes in Bakarganj, as the dispossessed landlord inevitably fought back with all the force at his disposal.

Direct resistance to the landlords was organised by the leaders of the puritanical Faraizi movement. The Faraizis had been founded in 1830 by Haji Shariatullah, who after returning from Mecca began a campaign against traditional religious practices that contradicted the teachings of the Quran. The movement's political element grew out of his instructions to stop paying taxes to landlords for the worship of Hindu gods. Under Shariatullah's son, Dudu Mian, the Faraizis also supported the cultivators in disputes over rent and tenure conditions. Despite their activities, however, the balance of power in the Sundarbans—money and muscle, the courts and the police—remained with the landlords.

The deforestation of the Bakarganj Sundarbans had brought big profits to the government, to the landlords, and especially to the middlemen. The labourers and cultivators had been left exposed to the storm-waves of the Bay of Bengal. Their exposure was inseparable from their position at the bottom of the tenure chain. Again it was the poorest people, with the fewest choices about where to live and what work to do, who were at the greatest risk of disaster.

3

THE CYCLONE

Towards the end of October 1876 there were a few days of complete calm over the Bay of Bengal. The south-west monsoon was over; the north-east monsoon was yet to begin. The weather stations along the coast were recording high air pressures, low temperatures, and light winds. The skies were unclouded. It was, the meteorologist John Elliott later wrote, 'as near an approach to an almost perfect equilibrium of meteorological conditions and actions ... as probably ever obtains'.

It was also the season of storms. The cyclone formed in the south of the bay, near the Nicobar Islands. On 30 October it began its passage north. The commander of the *British Sceptre* had been expecting bad weather, and on the evening of 30 October saw there was a storm coming. Big banks of cloud were building up; the moon was shining with a reddish glare, touching the clouds the same colour. From the south and south-east there was a high, rolling swell. The storm arrived that night. By morning the waves were rising in peaks. Sheets of lightning flashed in the sky; the wind came in blasts; the rain fell in hot and cold torrents. Soon the wind was 'one continuous roar'. The ship's lee side was underwater, and the mast looked as though it might go at any moment. And then it was over. 'Thank God!' the commander wrote in his log. 'Centre is passed.'

When it overtook the *Tennyson* the cyclone was travelling at a rate not often exceeded by storms in the Bay of Bengal. It passed over the ship with 'a roar like thunder', throwing it on its beam ends and sweeping away everything on deck. A few hours later it was the turn of the *Lightning*. 'Blowing furiously, impossible to stand against the wind', the commander wrote. 'Rains like a fire-pump hose, blinding and overpowering; sails blowing away from the yards. Men refuse to go aloft to pass extra gaskets, neither could they go. The atmosphere a perfect foggy foam; men can do nothing but hold on for self-protection.' When the commander went to secure the quarter boat he was lifted 10 feet above the deck by a gust of wind; when he came down he was knocked senseless, saved only by the length of rope he had been holding on to.

The last ship to meet the cyclone on its passage up the bay was the steamer *Moulmein*, crossing from Chittagong to Calcutta. The stormy weather arrived on the morning of 31 October. The captain sent the passengers into the saloon and battened down the forehatch. At 5:00 p.m. the topmast was blown away, and at 7:00 p.m. the foremast followed. The funnel broke off and rolled overboard; the fires went out and the boiler ran dry. The lowest reading of the barometer was taken at 8:00 p.m.; the cyclone was passing to the east, 40 or 50 miles away. It was travelling faster than ever, and it still had some way to go before it reached the mouth of the Meghna.

On the night of 31 October the lowest parts of the coast and the islands were flooded by an unusually high bore. This first flood did little serious damage. But it was only a forerunner of the great wave that was to come. The cyclone was bringing with it a mass of water that had been drawn up by its low air pressure and circling winds. When it reached the shallow bed of the estuary this mass of water piled up into an immense wave. It was met by the waters of the Meghna trying to find an exit to the sea. The river and the wave fought each other over the shallows; the wave grew higher and higher; and then it advanced.

For days afterwards there were reports from ships out in the bay of an unusual debris floating by: uprooted trees, cattle carcasses, house roofs and furniture, and a great number of dead bodies.

॰ॶ

On the night of 31 October a strong gale—'apparently the tail of a cyclone'—passed over Dacca. It did little damage. On 4 November it was mentioned by Frederick Peacock, the divisional commissioner of Dacca, in a routine dispatch. There had been no reports of damage from the other districts of the division—no reports, even, from Bakarganj.

Usually it took two or three days for a letter to get from Barisal, the headquarters town of Bakarganj, to Dacca. But this time it was taking longer. 'All yesterday the sky was overcast with dull leaden clouds, which clearly prognosticated bad weather', the collector Ebenezer Barton wrote on 1 November. At 3:00 p.m. that day a brisk breeze had come up, and rain had started to fall. By 11:00 p.m. the breeze had become a violent storm. Barton got out of bed at 1:00 a.m. and watched the storm until 4:30 a.m., when it began to subside. In the morning he went out to survey the damage to the town and its neighbourhood. Buildings and trees had been brought to the ground, but no deaths had been reported. The question was what had happened in the south of the district. For most of the night Barton had felt the wind blowing from the north, which gave him reason to hope that the coast had escaped. If there had been a wave, though, he knew that 'the loss inflicted by this wind would have been as nothing'.

Barton didn't have to wait long for his fears to be confirmed. On 2 November one of his deputies, Tajammal Ali, returned from char Fennah Baher, an island to the north-east of Barisal. It was one of the government's resumed estates; Ali had been there on settlement duty. He had been lying asleep in his boat when the wave came. The boat had been wrecked. Wading up to his neck in water, the wind roaring around him, he had found a silk-cotton tree and climbed up it. In the morning, as the water was going down, he had seen bodies floating by.

This was the first Barton had heard of the storm-wave. Things had obviously gone badly in the north-east of the district: he could now understand the meaning of the silence from the south. A far deadlier and more destructive wave must have overtaken the Sundarbans divisions of Golachipa and Bauphal, and also the islands in the estuary: Dakhin Shahbazpur, Manpura, Badura, and all the others.

The next morning Deenanath Sarkar arrived at Barisal in a small, barely watertight boat. Sarkar was sub-inspector of police at Daulatkhan, the subdivisional headquarters of Dakhin Shahbazpur. The story he told Barton is almost incredible. But the wave had not left much room for ordinary stories: the only ones who had experienced it and didn't have a similar story to tell were the dead.

'I was present at the station on the night of 31 October when the storm commenced. At about 11:00 p.m. a small house belonging to a mooktar [attorney] caught fire. Our attention was directed in that quarter, when we suddenly found that water was gradually rising under our feet. Then we saw the water rushing towards us. When we saw this, we lost all hope. I attempted to go on to the top of the roof of the guard-house, but was unable to go there on account of the great rush of the water. With great difficulty some of us scrambled up on top of the prisoners' work-shed. The water began to rise up to the work-shed roof, where we had perched ourselves. It rose so rapidly that the roof was carried along by the stream. We were about six or seven of us who held on to the roof, which was even carried over some trees.'

The roof then broke apart. Sarkar tried to swim, but could feel himself being carried away. A waterlogged country boat came by: it was a piece of luck. He and two or three others, one of them a prisoner he had just released from the lock-up, got hold of it and climbed in. But the boat didn't last long; again he ended up in the water. And again he had a piece of luck. This time it was an uprooted silk-cotton tree. Whipped up and down by the waves, the thorny branches of the silk-cotton cut him up badly. When it drifted into an orchard of mango, coconut, and betel nut trees he let go. The rest of the night he spent in the branches of a mango tree.

By 8:30 a.m. the water had fallen enough for Sarkar to come down. He began calling out to see if anyone else was in the garden. A young constable and another man were there, both clinging to trees. Govinda Das, a head constable, was nearby. Together they set out for the subdivisional headquarters. A man sitting on the thatched roof of his house told them where the road was. They had lost all sense of direction. The young constable had a small piece of cloth around his waist; the rest were naked. They picked up some floating rags to cover themselves. Soon they reached Daulatkhan. 'I could not recognise the place', Sarkar said. It had been buried under 30 feet of water. Its buildings had been washed away, and many of its inhabitants had disappeared. Sarkar helped himself to a handful of wet rice from a sack in the bazaar, found a boat, and set off for Barisal.

On 4 November, the day after Sarkar's arrival, Barton received a report from Umacharan Banerjee. Banerjee was the subdivisional officer of Dakhin Shahbazpur. Unlike Sarkar, he couldn't remember what had happened to him on the night of the storm. 'How I was carried away, or how I was afterwards saved, is more than I can say.' When he regained consciousness he found that every one of his twelve children and grandchildren had been drowned. In the subdivision as a whole, he guessed, 10,000 people and 50,000 cattle had been washed away. He couldn't even guess how much property had been destroyed. People had lost their houses, their boats, their savings. 'My jewels, my cash, my furniture, my books, my clothes, my everything have gone.' Of most immediate concern, there was no rice, dal, or any other food available.

News of the great disaster was now arriving almost hourly from officials in the southern parts of the district. As Barton suspected, the coast of Patuakhali subdivision had also been flooded. On the night of the storm De Silva, a sub-registrar at Bauphal, had climbed a big jack tree in his compound with eight others; in the morning he had come down with two others from a different tree. Jackson, the sub-inspector of police at Golachipa, had turned up at the subdivisional headquarters with his body 'cut into a hundred ways' and his wife and children dead. The exact details of what had happened were not yet clear. But the reports of the lower officials suggested that the scale of the calamity was unprecedented. The question now was how Barton would respond to it.

❧

As soon as Barton heard from Tajammal Ali about the wave in the north-east he sent him back with small amounts of rice, dal, and cash for the survivors. Other deputy collectors were sent out with similar amounts to Manpura, off the coast of Dakhin Shahbazpur, and to the southern divisions of Golachipa and Bauphal. H.N. Harris, the superintendent of police, was put in charge of relief work on Dakhin Shahbazpur itself. All were given instructions to distribute food and money only in cases of absolute necessity.

This was on 2 November. The next day, after hearing from Sarkar, Barton decided that Dakhin Shahbazpur was going to need more than the Rs. 460 that Harris had been given. George Kerry, a Baptist missionary at Barisal, left immediately with a boatload of rice and another Rs. 500. Two 'native doctors' (Indian doctors trained in Western medicine) were dispatched, and several minor officials from the collectorate were sent down with food, money, and clothes to establish a network of relief centres on the island.

These measures were taken without Peacock's permission. There was no telegraph at Barisal, and no railway either. A reply to a letter sent to Dacca would take at least a week. In the course of that week any number might die for want of relief. Barton knew that if help was to be given it would have to be immediate. Waiting on orders from above would be 'a dereliction of duty ... and most probably an imperilling of the lives of people ... whom a little timely relief might have saved'.

It was one thing to decide to act, another to actually do so. The logistical difficulties were extreme. Relief workers and supplies could only be transported by water, but most of the boats in Barisal had been wrecked by the storm. Even when boats were available, crews often were not: many boatmen had drowned, and the survivors were busy rebuilding their huts. Along with the lack of transport went a lack of information. Barton still had very little idea of what had happened on the coast of the mainland, and no news at all from the south of Dakhin Shahbazpur.

The earliest news of the disaster had been brought to Barisal by officials working in the mofussil. Soon the relief officers sent from the town itself began submitting their reports. Harris was the highest-ranking of these officers, and his views were given special attention. Travelling to Daulatkhan he had passed corpses and carcasses floating in the river and laid out along both sides of the island. He had also passed boatloads of the living, home-less people in desperate need of food and clothing. At Daulatkhan the smell from the corpses was 'perfectly unbearable': the air had been 'poisoned'. People were crowding in from the surrounding countryside, clamouring for food; but there was no rice for sale, let alone for relief. The shopkeepers had fled. A shopkeeper's assistant had sent a boat away for rice, but that would not feed everyone. The boats had been destroyed and the bamboo bridges over the creeks washed away; even those who had money couldn't get to a market where food might be available. Harris thought the government would have to intervene. 'It is very doubtful whether any rice will be able to get here for the present by private enterprise.'

Barton agreed. 'We have come to the conclusion', he wrote to Peacock, 'that in order to save the distressed tracts from depopulation relief on a considerable scale is absolutely necessary.' He proposed that 50,000 maunds of rice (a maund was about 80 pounds, or a gunny sack of rice), 12,000 maunds of dal, 1000 maunds of mustard oil, and 1000 maunds of salt be sent to the south of the district. Around Rs. 100,000 would be spent on rebuilding the roads, digging new tanks, and building embankments. Relief would be given in the usual manner: freely to the destitute and those unable to work, and in return for labour to the able-bodied. And it would be given sparingly. The point of the scheme was to keep people from dying, not to help them recover their livelihoods. It was assumed that they could manage that on their own. From the government they would get 'only as much as is barely sufficient to maintain them in life'. The important thing was that they get something, and soon.

Barton had so far done everything he could with the resources he had access to. He had even come up with a plan for resources that were not yet available to him. But in practical terms this was not all that much. And he had still heard nothing from Peacock in Dacca. The stress was beginning to tell. 'I have been in a state of great mental anxiety, which has been increased by the limited resources at my disposal for the relief of distress, and by the isolation of this district, which makes it impossible for me to get orders from you or from Calcutta within a week.'

The seriousness of the situation was made even clearer by George Kerry's first report. Kerry had left for Daulatkhan on 4 November. It had been a slow journey downriver: his boat was fully laden, low in the water, and at risk of grounding on a char. On leaving Barisal he had seen only 'the ordinary signs of devastation by a severe storm'. But it was different the next morning. The chars along the river were lined with people crying out for something to eat, 'wild with the excitement of desire for food'. They told Kerry that they were dying of hunger. Kerry left small amounts of rice, dal, and salt: there wasn't much else he could do. Everywhere there were dead bodies. 'I stopped writing just now to look upon a hundred or more cattle lying dead, with the bodies of dead men and women lying here and there among them.'

When night came Kerry's boatmen anchored in a creek to avoid the bore. Kerry used the time to distribute relief. He found that the people had been living on the unripe fruit of their broken plantain trees. When he tried to leave in the morning other people, 'mad for food and salt', tried to stop him. The rest of the journey to Daulatkhan was like a journey through the underworld: for the last 10 miles the river was lined with corpses. 'This terrible calamity is something frightful to think of, and I only see a small part of it.'

The next day he reached Tozamuddin, in the very south of Dakhin Shahbazpur. It was the most isolated part of an isolated district. Nobody had heard anything from it since the cyclone. Kerry found the few survivors living in the ruins of their houses, subsisting on rotten rice. Salt was in great demand: without it they couldn't get themselves to eat the damaged rice that was left, or the unripe fruit, stem, and roots of the plantain tree. Kerry's recommendation to Barton was simple and unqualified: 'large supplies must be sent to them with all speed'. Sail and row boats, he saw after his own slow journey, wouldn't be enough—there would have to be river steamers, and they would have to be 'laden with grain, salt, and cloth'.

Even where rice was available, shopkeepers were putting up prices or keeping it from sale to make as much profit from the disaster as possible. Ohiduddin Mahomed, a collectorate clerk who had been sent to Dakhin Shahbazpur on relief duty, found the shopkeepers of Gazipur selling their rice and salt at 'a terribly high rate'. Arguing with them had little effect, so he asked Barton to arrange for traders from other places to send food to the island. Barton was willing to intervene in the market in this way, but had little success in actually doing so: the grain dealers of Barisal bazaar had already combined to raise their prices, and refused to send their assistants to the south in case they were looted.

Mahomed's example indicates that the relief work was not being done by Europeans alone. But the Bengali officials were not given the same level of responsibility as Harris and Kerry. Ananda Sen, a deputy collector who knew Dakhin Shahbazpur better than any other official, was only Harris's assistant on the island. This peculiarity reflected the structure of the Indian civil service, which was virtually closed to Indians themselves. In 1876 there were only a handful of covenanted Indian officers, none of whom had charge of a district. Indians were considered to be politically and morally untrustworthy, and had been excluded from the upper levels of the administration as a matter of policy since the Company's rise to power in the eighteenth century. Despite pronouncements of equality after the Crown took over in 1858, in practice this exclusion continued. Some of the consequences of rewarding race over competence would become clear as the disaster unfolded.

Through an 'unfortunate postal blunder', no news at all of the cyclone and storm-wave reached Peacock in Dacca until the evening of 6 November. The next day six more letters arrived, and Peacock learnt of the disaster that had overtaken Bakarganj. He was more upset about Barton's proposed relief plan than about the calamity itself. The relief work that had been done so far had been paid for out of the Barisal treasury, but Barton's enlarged plan would go well beyond local funds. And this was a problem. After reading the letters from Barton, with their enclosures from Harris and Kerry, Peacock decided that Barton had over-reacted. 'I am inclined to think', he told the secretary to the government of Bengal, 'that the collector has taken an exaggerated view of the extent to which relief will be necessary.'

It was an extraordinary statement, unsupported by any reasoning. Barton's plan was based on the best available information. He had made it clear that the full extent of the disaster hadn't yet been determined: more might be needed, certainly not less. Peacock had no information of his own: he was reacting to the financial imperatives of empire, not to the disaster in Bakarganj.

Barton had asked for 50,000 maunds of rice; Peacock sent 4000. The collector of Dacca, David Lyall, was told to organise the shipment. Lyall knew that the only rice getting to Barisal from Dacca had been organised by local families—presumably wealthy ones—to feed their relatives, and that rice from merchants was mostly going to the port town of Chittagong, not the remote parts of Bakarganj. Still he told Peacock that he thought no more help would be needed. 'It appears likely that the distress will be only temporary, and that private enterprise will do all after the first difficulty is overcome.'

Already there were signs of divergence in the official response to the cyclone. The local officials in Bakarganj had the only reliable information about the disaster. But they were being overruled by their superiors at the higher levels of the administration, whose main concern was with the government's finances. The recommendation that the government should provide relief was countered by an assumption that private enterprise would be able to supply the people's needs. It was this assumption—a badly mistaken one—that would eventually form the basis of the government's relief policy.

CR

On the other side of the estuary the collector of Noakhali, Reginald Porch, didn't have to wait to find out whether there had been a storm-wave. Sudharam, he reported the next day, had suffered 'a two-fold calamity'. First there had been the wind, which blew until 4:00 a.m. Then, half an hour later, there had been cries that the sea was coming in. The advancing wave sounded like the bore coming up the Meghna. But this wave wasn't confined to the river, and the streets of the bazaar were soon running with water. In the morning Porch went out to inspect the damage. 'The whole place now wears quite a wintry aspect', he wrote, 'and looks as though it had been cannonaded and then inundated—nothing could exceed the desolation.'

If the wave had reached this far inland its effects in the more exposed parts of the district must have been terrible. Yet just as in Bakarganj, information about what had happened beyond the town was hard to come by. The big islands on the Noakhali side of the estuary—Hatia and Sandwip—were even more isolated from the headquarters town of Sudharam than Dakhin Shahbazpur was from Barisal. On 2 November Porch sent a police officer, Harish Chowdhury, to Hatia to see whether the cyclone had created any need for relief measures—a peculiar choice of words, as there could hardly have been any doubt that it had. Other officials were sent with provisions to the government's estates of Bamni and Siddhi, and the manager of Bhulua, a huge estate under the government's Court of Wards, was told to send supplies to the chars along the coast.

The first flood on the night of 31 October had been the unusually high salt-water bore of the Chittagong tide. A few people had drowned when their houses collapsed or their boats were wrecked, but most had been able to get up a tree or onto a roof. One person taken by surprise was the Noakhali postmaster, moored in a creek about 10 miles inland from the Meghna. He was woken just before midnight by the cries of his boatmen; looking up, he saw the crest of the wave gleaming in the moonlight. He got hold of a lifebelt before the boat capsized, and spent the rest of the night paddling in the water: his boatmen clung on to the spars.

The second flood, the storm-wave, came a few hours before daybreak. Its depth and force varied across the estuary. The size of the channel, the direction of the wind, and the timing of the ordinary tide all affected its progress. In some places the flood was as low as 10 feet; in others it reached heights of 40 feet. In some places it came on in a rush, and in others it rose gradually. A man from a char near Sandwip told of his narrow escape. 'I saw a large mass of water like the bore coming up the river as high as the tree I was on. I expected to be soon swept away by this water, but the wind suddenly came down from the north. It looked dark as it dashed against the wave, and both wind and wave stood still for a time opposed to each other, and the wave rose up and then fell back, driven by the wind to the sea.' Many who saw the wave didn't live to tell their story. The dead bodies, cattle carcasses, and broken houses were carried onto the mainland, and taken back out to sea when the waters flowed off in the morning.

The first few days after the storm, as news came in and relief went out, are not as well-documented for Noakhali as they are for Bakarganj. The government of Bengal's printed proceedings are dominated by events in Bakarganj: there are fewer letters from Porch or his subordinates. But the Noakhali district records for 1876 and 1877, kept at the National Archives of Bangladesh in Dhaka, go some way towards filling the gap. (The volumes for Bakarganj and Chittagong have disappeared.) With one exception, though—a volume of letters from the subdivisional officer of Feni—they contain only copies of Porch's correspondence. The letters from the officials he sent out to investigate the damage and provide relief, and those he received from his superiors, have not been preserved.

The contents of the missing letters can sometimes be inferred from Porch's replies. By 5 November he obviously had enough information to know that he was dealing with a major disaster. That day a message was sent to Calcutta from the telegraph station at Comilla, north of Noakhali. 'Great loss of life on coast and islands. Fearful distress for food and water. Relief sent, expenditure being made in anticipation of sanction. Cholera has broken out. Steamer, food, and medicine urgently required.' The next day another message was sent, this time with more precise instructions. 'Send steamer quickly from Dacca or elsewhere with five thousand maunds rice, and fifty maunds salt, and as much drinking water as possible.'

At the same time Porch was mobilising the resources available to him around the town. He had already set one of his deputies, Kalinath Bose, to work finding boats, bullock carts, and men for relief work. It wasn't an easy job. The shortage of boats was even worse in Sudharam than it was in Barisal, and most would-be relief workers were busy rebuilding their homes. Bose was also asked to try to secure 1000 maunds of rice and 100 maunds of salt. This had to be done tactfully: the last thing Porch wanted was to turn the people against the weakened administration.

News from Sandwip reached the commissioner of Chittagong, Alexander Smith, before it reached Porch. On 3 November twenty-four people, mostly women, had turned up at Smith's compound in Chittagong. They had been carried to the Chittagong coast from Sandwip, across an arm of the sea at least

10 miles wide, on the roofs of houses or pieces of wood. One woman had had to let two of her children drown to save herself. Smith thought he would wait for more information to come in before he decided what would be needed in the way of relief. (He did, however, send a boat with a little rice.) Whatever help was decided on, he hoped it wouldn't be needed for long.

The collector of Chittagong, John Veasey, felt the same peculiar optimism about the prospects of the town and district. The town had suffered badly from the wind, and the wave, though not nearly as high as in the Meghna estuary, had swept away many houses. There had been serious damage to the shipping at the port. Three quarters of the rice stored in the merchants' godowns along the riverbank had been spoilt, and chests of tea worth Rs. 40,000 were floating in the river. The government's salt storehouses, containing 70,000 maunds of salt, had been wrecked. The poorest inhabitants of the town were eating the fermenting rice that had been thrown up, along with many corpses, on the foreshore; the smell had made the streets impassable. Yet the municipal commissioners, at a meeting on 3 November, decided not to spend more than Rs. 500 on relief; and by 4 November Veasey had spent only Rs. 50. Ending his report on a familiar note, he expressed a hope that the full sum, small as it was, would not be needed; the people, he thought, should be able to get by 'with little or no assistance'.

Veasey was already unpopular among the people of Chittagong, and his behaviour after the storm-wave—which he insisted on calling a 'high tide'—did nothing to improve his reputation. 'He was never blessed with an over-sweet temper,' the *Hindoo Patriot*'s Chittagong correspondent wrote, 'and the late events have soured it to vinegar. A thin emaciated appearance, a vine-gared face with a scowl lurking in one of its corners, slightly lame in one of his legs ... and jolting most unhappily on his pony, you have the figure of Mr. J.C. Veasey, whom you have only to look at to think that he is coming to bite you.' The unprepossessing exterior was matched by a notably cynical attitude towards the victims of the cyclone. Instead of trying to establish the number of deaths and the loss of property, Veasey was 'straining every nerve to under-rate the calamity'; instead of coming up with a relief plan, he was carrying on with the revenue settlement work.

The worst-affected areas of Chittagong district were those to the north of the town. There were worrying reports from the pilgrimage centre of Sitakund, where two or three thousand people had been attending a Hindu religious festival. Veasey, however, was not inclined to believe the stories that were coming in of mass death. 'Natives invariably have very loose ideas as to numbers,' he wrote, 'and though the loss of life may have been considerable, it is certain it cannot have been anything approaching what it is said to have been.' This was hardly a sound basis for planning an effective response to disaster. But it was a widespread attitude among British officials, and one that was to result in much suffering.

Another widespread attitude was that the government's spending on relief should be kept as low as possible. Back in Noakhali Porch's relief scheme was certainly proceeding along these lines. His ideas about how the responsibility for relief should be assigned can be found in his instructions to Sarada Sarkar, the subdivisional officer of Feni. 'The police should see that the people help one another where able. The zamindars should especially be required to do their duty in this respect. You should raise subscriptions for this purpose—the amount will be supplemented from the treasury here. You should expend the money in judicious relief through the high police officers, keeping account of the same. Rice may be sold to those who can pay or given gratuitously to those in want or without any means.'

The plan, then, was that most of the relief work would be done by the people themselves, by their landlords, and (in the form of subscriptions) by the wealthier residents of the district. Government funds were to be only a supplement. Yet the government was one of the largest landlords in the district, and its estates—the chars—were those that had suffered most from the storm-wave. The other landlords were notoriously apathetic about the well-being of their tenants, and unlikely to have a sudden change of heart when financial help was needed. The district had few rich residents from whom to solicit subscriptions. The markets were in disarray. And the victims of the cyclone, who had in many instances been left without food, fresh water, shelter, crops, cattle, or money, were hardly in a position to act as the agents of their own relief, with or without the promptings of the police.

Barton had asked for 50,000 maunds of rice and 1000 of salt; Porch asked for 5000 maunds of rice and 50 of salt. Barton might not have got what he wanted, but the divergence between the two estimates is striking. Barton's letters are those of an officer of energy, independent judgement, and a sense of duty to the people of his district; Porch's are those of a man looking over his shoulder at his superiors, rather than at the victims of disaster in front of him. That difference might well have been reflected in the amount and effectiveness of relief distributed in the first week after the storm. As the situation came under the control of the higher authorities, though, there would be much less room for local initiative.

⟨⟩

The government's response to the cyclone was shaped—and complicated—by the effects of disaster on the local administration. One immediate problem was a shortage of personnel. The ranks of the police had been thinned, and a number of clerks and other minor officials had been lost. At Daulatkhan the native judge, the sub-registrar, the postmaster, the clerk of the land records, the court sub-inspector, and the excise officer had all been drowned. Many of those who survived were unable or unwilling to get back to work. Ishan Biswas, sub-inspector of police on Hatia, left the island after losing his entire family, citing his 'miserable condition of body and mind' as the reason for his departure.

Much government property had been lost or damaged during the storm. Government buildings that had only been exposed to the wind were, by virtue of their superior construction, usually still standing. But most of the buildings exposed to the wave had collapsed. All that remained of the Bauphal sub-registrar's office was his chair, which he found next morning in a nearby field. The greatest loss had been at Daulatkhan, where even the masonry buildings, among them the subdivisional cutcherry— the main administrative office—had been destroyed.

With the government buildings had gone the government records. These were as powerful a symbol of authority as any building, and from a practical point of view of much greater importance. Harris did what he could to retrieve the waterlogged books, records, and registers that had ended up in tanks and gardens around Daulatkhan, but most wouldn't be seen again. The loss of the Daulatkhan records was replicated on a smaller scale all over the wave-affected areas. Tajammal Ali, who nearly drowned when his boat was capsized, lost his settlement papers, his testimonials of service, his copies of the regulations, and his books—among them Henry Beveridge's history of Bakarganj, published earlier that year and lent to him by Beveridge's successor, Barton.

There were also problems with the maintenance of law and order. In the days after the cyclone there were several reports of looting. Harris, in Daulatkhan, heard that a storehouse containing gold and silver ornaments and stocks of rice had been robbed by 'a band of turbulent Mahommedans'. Crimes were also being committed by other 'bad characters'; a head constable had been beaten when he had tried to put a stop to looting in the town bazaar. One consolation, Harris wrote, was that the subdivisional treasure chest was safely buried under the bricks and mortar of the cutcherry ruins.

In Chittagong town there were no reports of looting, or even of petty theft. But in Sitakund it was said that corpses were being stripped of their clothes and jewellery, and that property washed out of houses was being plundered. In Noakhali, Porch reported, gangs with cudgels, billhooks, and hatchets were going around the flooded areas, breaking open and taking whatever they could—whether or not the owners were present. There were also rumours of bodies being found with their hands and feet missing, having been robbed of their ornaments after death.

The districts along the coast of Bengal had long been regarded by the British as unusually prone to lawlessness and crime. 'The general moral character of the inhabitants', one of the early magistrates of Bakarganj wrote, 'is at the lowest pitch of infamy ... there is no species of fraud or villainy the higher classes will not be guilty of, and to these crimes in the lower classes may be added murder, robbery, theft, wounding, &c., on the slightest occasion. In fact it is hardly going too far in asserting that the whole of the inhabitants of this district are dacoits.' Henry Parker, secretary to the Board of Customs, Salt and Opium, thought that such characteristics were typical of frontier societies. 'Everywhere people dwelling on the frontiers of great forests, the pioneers before whose hatchets these forests recede, people who dwell in islands surrounded by broad and dangerous rivers, or on the sea-shore, are noted ... for hardihood and roughness of character.' Even in the 1870s the people of the chars and forest clearings were thought to have a special predisposition to crime.

Many of the developments in the administration of the seaboard districts had been made in response to this lawlessness, which threatened the Company's trade as well as its land revenue. The first police stations in Bakarganj had been set up along the banks of the rivers to protect the Company's trading boats from dacoits. (They were not there to protect the people of the district: Beveridge's history suggests that the depredations of the Company's servants did as much to disturb the trade of Bakarganj as any dacoits.) And Noakhali's first magistrate had been appointed to prevent dacoities on the new chars in the estuary so that resumption proceedings could go ahead.

A reputation for lawlessness, reports of looting, a weakened administration—it was for these reasons that the restoration of the state's power came to dominate relief work in 1876. All officials agreed that strengthening the police was the first priority. Harris, in Daulatkhan, asked for a European police officer and a large number of Indian subordinates to stop the plundering. Veasey, in Chittagong, showed rare energy in posting guards around the merchants' godowns. Porch told his superintendent of police to provisionally fill any vacancies, and let him know if he had any ideas for further strengthening the force.

Some of the looting that went on in the immediate aftermath of the storm would have been the work of professional criminal gangs, of which there were many along the coast. Chars Balamara and Monasha in Noakhali, for instance, were home to dacoits whose ancestors were said to have bought their tenures with the proceeds of their crimes. The breakdown of law and order even allowed a few members of the police to join in the plunder—two officers on Hatia were found with other people's silver ornaments in their possession. But some of the looting was also related to food scarcity and the lack of relief. In Daulatkhan people raided the shops in the bazaar. In Tozamuddin a trader with a large supply of rice was forced by a hungry crowd to give some of it away. And on 12 November a dozen men from Hatia, which hadn't yet received any help from the mainland, robbed a trader's boat while he was waiting for the tide to turn.

None of the officials connected the looting to the scarcity of food after the cyclone. They saw it only as evidence of a dangerous vacuum of authority—a return to the disturbed conditions of the eighteenth and early nineteenth centuries. And this demanded a firm response. 'Relief', in these circumstances, would be as much about saving the state as about preserving the lives of its subjects.

CR

The cyclone had not been indifferent to social divisions. Its effects on Barisal, the headquarters town of Bakarganj, showed how capably it could distinguish between rich and poor. Like the other mofussil towns of Bengal, Barisal was small and sparsely populated. Its main business was government: many of its inhabitants were officials or lawyers. The other class in the town was made up of the servants of these professional men. Most of the women were from the servant class, and a large number were prostitutes. There were few middle-class women: most of the lawyers and officials, and even the traders and shopkeepers, preferred to make their homes outside the district.

The wealthier residents of Barisal generally lived in pucka houses of solid brick, raised above the ground on low arches. The rest of the town made do in ramshackle huts or cutcha houses of mat and thatch. When the wind came up the poorer townspeople realised that their flimsy houses were not going to last the night. The light of the full moon allowed many of them to make an escape. They knew very well where to find shelter, and 'fled in thousands to the nearest pucka houses'. Others spent the night exposed to the wind and rain, and to the dangers of falling trees and flying debris. When Barton went out in the morning to survey the damage to the town he found that nine tenths of the huts and cutcha houses had been brought down by the wind. The pucka houses had some damage to their doors and windows, and some plaster peeled off their walls, but not one had collapsed.

The same pattern of destruction and preservation could be seen in Sudharam, the headquarters town of Noakhali. Houses of mat and thatch were brought down, but houses made of brick remained standing. The survival strategy was the same too: the poor people headed straight for the nearest pucka buildings. 'Those on the south-west', Porch explained, 'fled to the tank house and to the other brick buildings in the neighbourhood ... Those on the south-east were sheltered in the circuit house.'

There was also a connection between class and exposure to disaster in Chittagong town. The town site, on the banks of the Karnaphuli river, was dotted all over with small, steep hills. The houses of the British officials and their families were built on these hills, as were the government buildings and the houses of the wealthiest Bengali residents. The rest of the town's inhabitants lived in the hollows between the hills, at risk of floods, landslides, and (it was believed) fever from the nearby chars. Most of the cutcha houses in the 'native town' were blown down or unroofed by the wind, and those near the river were swept away by the wave. A few families in the Portuguese quarter found refuge in the sturdy Roman Catholic church.

Beyond the administrative towns pucka buildings were few and far between. Brick was a sign of power and wealth, and people of power and wealth didn't live along the coast. 'All the zamindars ... are absentees,' Henry Beveridge wrote of Dakhin Shahbazpur, 'and there is hardly a pakka house on the island.' The only exceptions were the temples and mosques, which were usually well-built and raised above the ground on solid earthen plinths. On the night of the storm these provided a refuge for villagers lucky enough to be living nearby. The subdivisional officer of Patuakhali, Krishna Gupta, found shelter along with many others on the crowded veranda of an old temple. Little else in the neighbourhood was left standing.

Most of the cyclone's victims lived in the forest clearings of the Bakarganj Sundarbans or on the islands and chars of the estuary. The names of the worst-affected places are familiar from the resumption proceedings and the title deeds of the forest grants: Rangabali, Bara and Chota Basdia, Manpura, Nalchira, Siddhi, Badu. Their inhabitants had been exposed to great risk for the profit of the government and the landlords, and that risk had now become reality. Their mat and thatch houses had given them no protection. The plinths that the houses rested on had been built for much lower floods. People who managed to get onto their roofs were usually swept away on them and drowned. Most of the survivors had climbed or been caught in the branches of a tree; many had terrible scratches from the thorns of the silk-cotton, which had dug into them and stopped them from being carried away.

Survival generally depended on the number of trees surrounding a homestead. Clearings that had been only partly deforested had higher survival rates than those on which deforestation was complete. And clearings or chars that had been settled for some time, and so were surrounded by fruit trees, had higher survival rates than those on which the trees hadn't yet grown to maturity. On the treeless char Bhuta, a government estate in the south of Dakhin Shahbazpur, over half of the people and 90 per cent of the cattle were carried away. The death rate on char Lakhi, also in the south of the island, was much lower: most of the estate was 'still covered by dense jungle', which had 'preserved the lives of many'. (In the district next to Bakarganj, Jessore, there was a wide band of forest between the sea and the settlements, and no damage at all from the wave.)

An isolated exception to the general desolation could be seen in the Magh settlements along the Bakarganj coast. The houses of the Maghs were built in the Burmese style, raised 10 or 15 feet above the ground on strong posts, and their settlements were surrounded by thick jungle. The jungle had been deliberately preserved to break the force of the wind and the water. The

Bengali cultivators began their clearings from the river's edge, where the land was highest; the Maghs began theirs inland, away from the river. The wave had reached its greatest height—40 feet—in the south of the district, but the forest was higher still. By holding back the worst of the wave, it had given the Maghs a chance of survival.

The boatmen of the estuary were more likely to die during a storm than anyone else. Yet they are almost entirely absent from the official records. They made up only a small part of the population, and unlike the cultivators contributed little to the government's revenue. Barton mentions that on the night of the storm the boatmen of Barisal, about a tenth of the town's population, 'abandoned their boats, and took refuge in the premises of the European residents, or wherever they could find shelter'. The superintendent of police at Chittagong reported that on the island of Kutubdia, although there had been no loss of life on shore, the fishing boats had been wrecked and the fishermen (who often worked at night) had been drowned. Neither the fishermen nor the boatmen were included in the official estimate of casualties from the storm: in the utilitarian reckoning of empire they were not even statistics.

Most of the landlords' agents probably survived: every year before the Durga puja festival (which in 1876 began on 23 September) they left for their homes in the north and stayed away for two or three months. The landlords of Bakarganj and Noakhali would suffer financially, but had escaped physical harm. When the cyclone struck they were, as usual, absent from their estates. The exception was P.M. Gasper, an Armenian zamindar who happened to be at Daulatkhan on the night of the storm. 'May the Lord have mercy on his soul,' one of his fellows remarked, 'even though he had none for others.'

CR

Whether a person survived the storm depended on their age and sex as well as their class and occupation. The great numbers of dead children were noted by officials in all three of the districts affected by the wave. On the Patuakhali islands 85 per cent of the boys and 90 per cent of the girls had drowned. Officials made no attempt to find out the ages of the adults—the only reference to old age is to the single victim of the cyclone in Patuakhali town, 'an old woman'—but there can be little doubt that the proportion of deaths among the old and disabled was higher as well.

The women of Bakarganj and Noakhali lived under the control of their fathers, husbands, or sons. Purdah, the practice of secluding the women of the household from strangers, arrived in Bengal with Islam. It was soon being observed by Hindu and Muslim alike. The puritanical Faraizi sect was especially strong in the south-eastern districts, and purdah was probably enforced more rigorously in Bakarganj and Noakhali than in any other part of Bengal. Women of all classes except the poorest stayed indoors. They didn't work in the fields, and they didn't go to the markets: the only women to be seen in public were the impoverished, wraith-like widows.

Purdah greatly restricted women's ability to earn money. After the decline of the cotton-spinning industry the only way that women could contribute to the household income was by husking rice. Their low economic position, and purdah itself, put them at risk even in ordinary circumstances. 'In Bakarganj', the police officer J.H. Reilly wrote, 'the owner of the homestead is sole arbiter and ruler, independent of every social restraint. If a man of bad temper, he often develops into a despot or domestic tyrant. This will explain how a man ... whose pride has been fostered by wifely homage, when returning home from a hard day's ploughing, and finding his rice uncooked or cold, seizes a club or a knife, and either batters or hacks his wife to death.'

Early reports suggested that many more women had died in the cyclone than men. These impressions were confirmed after some basic statistics had been collected. On the islands off the Patuakhali coast 80 per cent of the women had died, as against 38 per cent of the men. On char Bhuta, in the south of Dakhin Shahbazpur, 276 women had died and 196 men. Striking as they are, these figures still do not show how disproportionately high the mortality rate among women was: in Bakarganj as a whole, and in the south especially, women were greatly outnumbered by men—in Patuakhali subdivision the sex ratio was 53 to 47, and in Golachipa it was 56 to 44.

The district officials were not especially interested in establishing the reasons for such a high death toll among women. It was assumed that it was the result of a difference in levels of physical strength, and there is no reason to think that this was not important. But the low social position of women must also have played a part. By making women reluctant to leave the house in search of shelter, purdah increased their chances of death. If they did leave the house—and there is evidence from Sudharam that some did—they would have been unable to swim or climb trees. They were also more likely to take responsibility for saving their children, although men tried to do this too.

In 1876 Nabin Sen was a deputy magistrate at Chittagong. The morning after the storm he went down with his commissioner to the banks of the Karnaphuli river. Just a few hours earlier people had been struggling for their lives in the water: now there were only corpses. 'Corpses and more corpses, and yet more corpses beyond, mingled with the carcasses of beasts and birds.' There was a mother with her child in her arms; a father who had tried to save his son and daughter by strapping them to himself with his dhoti; a husband who had tied himself to his wife. 'Oh God', Sen said afterwards. 'Is all that I saw truly Your handiwork?'

The victims of the storm-wave had not been randomly chosen: they had been part of a project of 'reclamation' that distributed risk and profit according to levels of wealth, status, and power. There were divisions of class and occupation, and there were divisions between men and women. In the end those divisions often separated the living from the dead. And the survivors were not out of trouble yet. Their future now was in the hands of those with access to resources and relief: the middle-class public, the zamindars, and the higher authorities.

4

THE RESPONSE

Sir Richard Temple could never have been accused of spending too much time at Belvedere, the Calcutta residence of the lieutenant governors of Bengal. He liked to see things for himself, and had made it his habit to spend the rainy season and autumn touring the province by boat. His launch was towed up and down the delta by a river steamer. He did his paperwork in its cabins, and used its long saloon and deck for receptions and balls. On special occasions the launch could even be illuminated—an island of luxury in the middle of the river, lighting up the night and the dark water surrounding it.

The districts at the mouth of the Meghna were on the itinerary of Temple's 1876 tour. Entirely by chance, he was already on his way to Noakhali when he heard of the disaster. He arrived there in his launch on the afternoon of 7 November. The district officials and a few prominent residents were at the river landing to meet him. That afternoon he was briefed on what had happened. He told Porch that the government wouldn't be able to spare a relief steamer, and sent a message to Dacca for five large boats, filled with supplies, to be sent down instead. It wasn't an encouraging start: Dacca boats, Porch explained to his commissioner, were not suitable for the dangerous waters of the estuary. If there was to be no steamer, though, they must get what they could.

By next morning word had spread that the lieutenant governor was on the scene. The station was crowded by destitute people, desperate for relief. Temple let them talk, but it was clear that he thought their views less reliable than his own. He had been in the district less than a day, but already he seemed to have all the answers. 'His Honour', Porch wrote in a typically long-winded report, 'made many inquiries from different people among the crowds that thronged the place, and hearing and answering the representations made, lucidly and authoritatively set forth to his hearers the utter impracticability of the measures that they were vainly harassing the local authorities by inconsiderately pressing.' It might almost have been supposed that it was Temple and the district officials who had been the real victims of the disaster.

The reception for Temple, which had been planned before the cyclone, was held that afternoon in the Sudharam circuit house. The address was read by Bagola Majumder, a landowner in government service. ('No flattery was too gross for Dicky Temple', one collector recalled: 'he believed it all'.) After the address Temple gave another speech about the disaster and the measures to be taken for its relief. Then, accompanied by his retinue, he left for Hatia to see first-hand the full effects of the storm.

Local officers knew that a tour by a 'great man' was likely to do more harm than good. 'Unless he is an exceptionally keen-sighted man', one wrote, 'he takes his superficial, hastily-formed impressions for real knowledge ... ever afterwards he is prone to refuse sanction to proposals submitted by the local officers, or to contradict their assertions, because of some erroneous impression he has imbibed on his hasty tour.' And this was precisely the result of Temple's tour of the coast in 1876.

After inspecting some of the cyclone-affected villages on Hatia, Dakhin Shahbazpur, and the Bakarganj mainland, Temple concluded that the people were recovering well on their own. At every homestead he visited he found the survivors busy drying their grain. They had shelter, 'little tent-like habitations' of sheets and clothes thrown over frameworks of broken branches. They were not in need of food, 'though there was naturally loud lamentation for their sorrows'. There were no signs of hunger. 'On the contrary, the noticeable circumstance was the trouble the people were taking to dry their grain.' He did not ask whether the people could have been drying their grain and still been hungry. His tour was only a means of justifying a predetermined course of action. The people who were claiming to be hungry, he decided, were actually those who had suffered the least and didn't need any help. 'The demeanour of those who really bore the brunt of the storm was marked by that enduring fortitude under suffering which distinguishes the native character.'

Temple's inspection resulted in a list of rules being issued to direct the local officials in their relief work. The first rule set the tone for the rest: 'Give relief in any case of proved or real necessity to save life, but try to avoid it, and I hope it will be generally avoidable.' The second rule was that any food relief should be sold, not given away. Markets were to be got up and running again, extra police were to be employed to stop plundering, and landlords were to take full responsibility for the welfare of their tenants. Applications for the remission of land revenue were to be ignored. The district administration, even in the worst-affected areas, was not to be interrupted. Relief was not going to be used to demonstrate the government's benevolence: as far as Temple was concerned, it was business as usual.

ᘓ

In refusing to allow any remission of the land revenue, Temple noted that 'no such thing was asked for, let alone granted, during the famine of 1874'. And it is Temple's experiences during that famine that provide the key to the uncompromising rules of 1876. The famine had begun with a drought in Bihar and north-western Bengal. It came after the horrors of the Orissa famine in 1866, when a million people had starved to death after the government refused to intervene. This time public and official opinion was firmly in favour of action. The government of Bengal was told that no human life should be lost that could by any means be saved. The lieutenant governor, Sir George Campbell, and Richard Temple were made responsible for organising relief work in consultation with the viceroy, Lord Northbrook. Temple was then financial member of the Imperial Legislative Council, but was understood to be Campbell's probable successor.

Campbell wanted the exportation of rice from Bengal to be stopped. But this went against the principles of political economy, and Northbrook, 'bred in the strictest sect of free traders', would not even consider it. ('I have no doubt', Campbell wrote in his memoirs, 'that in any other country than a British-governed country it would have been done.') It was decided to import food rather than to stop it being exported. Great quantities of rice were brought into the famine districts, mainly from Burma. Campbell knew that this was quite illogical: several million sterling had been spent on importing rice when a simple order stopping exports would have had the same effect. And the point of principle had hardly been won either, large-scale government imports being just as much of an interference with the ordinary course of trade as the prohibition of exports.

Temple had been supervising relief work as the government of India's 'famine delegate' since the beginning of 1874. To him the famine was just another chance to further his career, and in the hope of impressing the higher authorities he went well beyond the arrangements made by Campbell and the district collectors. 'In his usual theatrical way', one officer remembered, 'he rode at the rate of fifty or sixty miles a day through the districts, forming, as he said, an opinion on the condition of the people and the state of the crops ... he would sit down at night after one of these wild scampers and write a vainglorious minute, in which he stated that he ... had come to the conclusion that so many thousand maunds of grain (generally from three to four times as much as was really wanted) would be required to feed the people.'

The famine campaign was a success: only twenty-three deaths were recorded. It was the first time a famine in India had been met in a way that prevented serious mortality. But Temple's attempt to make his mark had also seen much money wasted, and his high-handed extravagance had given the free traders the chance they were looking for.

Temple's critics essentially claimed that the famine hadn't been real because it had been successfully averted. *The Economist*, in July 1874, thought that a serious famine would inevitably be followed by a loss of government revenue. The Indian finances showed that there had only been a slight decrease in the revenue. 'Where, then, it will be asked, is the famine?' *The Economist* might not have been able to find the famine, but it could find the spending on it easily enough. The importation of rice, it thought, had given Indians the idea that it was 'the duty of Government to keep them alive'. In trying to prevent famine deaths, 'we' (neither Temple nor Northbrook were mentioned by name, but *The Economist* wasn't implicating itself) had made 'many and great mistakes'; the worst of them was to have 'scattered money which ought to have been saved'.

The attack was continued in 1875 with the publication in Calcutta of an anonymous pamphlet by a member of the Bengal civil service. (It was shortly discovered that the author of the pamphlet was C.J. O'Donnell, brother of F.H. O'Donnell, the Irish nationalist MP.) The pamphlet maintained that nothing at all should have been spent on the 'so-called famine'; the whole thing had been invented by Temple to advance his own career.

The relief work had been 'an economic catastrophe, a culmination of unthrift and unreason', 'a demoralizing comedy on which the resources of the Empire have been squandered'. Northbrook, as viceroy, might have been technically responsible for the wastage, but his mistakes could be blamed on Temple's 'ignorance and incompetent counsel'.

The 'Black Pamphlet' was accurate enough in its estimation of Temple as a careerist of the highest order. His achievement, he wrote in his memoirs, had been 'in climbing rapidly up the steps of the ladder in a comparatively short time, and then in remaining at or near the top for the greater part of my official days'. He might have been able to take the criticism from the press and an anonymous subordinate in his stride. But the charge of extravagance had been brought up in Parliament too, and this was a real threat to his place 'at or near the top'. When he came upon his next calamity—the cyclone of 1876—he was ready to show that he deserved his position. 'It was fortunate that the first person who arrived on the scene should be myself', he later wrote. But fortunate for whom?

Temple had got into the habit of writing a long and detailed minute on virtually every issue that came before him. It helped him keep track of the reasoning behind his decisions, and gave him an outlet for what he fondly called his 'word-painting'. His minute on the cyclone of 1876 offers an explanation for the rules he had just issued to the local officials. The people who had been affected by the storm, he wrote, were very well off—'the richest peasantry in Bengal' (a statement that was far from true when applied to the inhabitants of the Sundarbans clearings and the chars). Those who had lost their assets still had substantial savings and credit. 'Soon, therefore, will boats come pouring in by the numerous channels from districts teeming with water-carriage; soon will fresh cattle be swum or ferried across the rivers from the overstocked districts of Eastern Bengal; soon will the grain bazars be re-opened, and the rustic marts be filled with the surplus produce of neighbouring tracts.' This reverie of market-driven recovery, though, was based on his assumption that the survivors were in a position to pay.

Temple had decided that the government's role in the recovery process would be as small as possible. He noted that the local authorities had opened relief centres, but assured his readers that relief was being given sparingly. 'We trust that very little relief will really be needed.' The relief centres, he explained, 'are as much for guard as for relief; are established for the purpose of restoring order, of preventing confusion, of keeping rustic society together, of making every responsible person stick to his work, and of ensuring that public confidence without which trade of all sorts cannot be quickly restored'. There was no mention of saving lives. That had been the policy in 1874, and it had got him into serious trouble. This time the government's expenses would be limited to the appointment of extra police and some advances to cultivators for new plough cattle. These expenses would not be beyond local, or at the worst provincial, funds. He did not expect to ask the government of India for any financial help at all.

Temple's free-market relief policy was a return to a familiar theory rather than a radical innovation. Laissez-faire was accepted by all levels of the Indian administration, and had been for generations. Almost every document on famine policy referred to the classical economic thought of Adam Smith or John Stuart Mill; just as influential was the population theory of Thomas Malthus, who had held the first chair of political economy at the East India Company's training college in England. Although free-market principles were occasionally modified in practice, they remained the natural point of departure. Temple's decision to keep the government's contribution to relief as small as possible and let the market take its course was unlikely to cause much controversy. It was, however, also unlikely to do much to help the victims of the cyclone.

☙

In the weeks after the cyclone it became clear that Temple, in his haste to wash his hands of the disaster, had badly underestimated the problems faced by the survivors. Laissez-faire was even less suitable as a response to a storm-wave than it was to a famine. People had lost not only their crops but also their homes, ploughs, bullocks, tools, and seeds: they simply had nothing to go on with.

Temple had seen during his tour that the survivors were salvaging whatever food they could. It was painstaking work. An official in Chittagong described how, when a pot containing rice was found, the ground nearby would be searched and the rice collected grain by grain. It would then be carefully washed, sifted, dried in the sun, and stored away again. The same would be done with other food. Most households had a small supply of rice and perhaps some chillies, betel nuts, and dried fish, but everything was more or less spoiled by the water.

This was hardly the impression given in Temple's minute, which described rice being taken out of underground storage pits as if it was the usual method of storing food along the coast. Some families might have kept a pot of rice underground in case of flood or fire, but by far the greatest part of the crop was kept in bamboo granaries outside their homes; one newspaper correspondent thought Temple had developed this misconception after seeing merchants in the bazaar lifting their stocks from beneath the floors of their shops.

In those parts of the seaboard that Temple had visited the crops had not been completely destroyed. The first and least violent flood of 31 October—the tidal bore—had covered the paddy with a layer of water that had protected it from the wind and the storm-wave that followed. In ordinary years the winter crop was much greater than local needs, and thousands of tonnes were exported to other districts. If this year only a third remained, Temple thought, it would still be enough for the local population. Temple's views were echoed by Krishna Gupta, the subdivisional officer of Patuakhali. Gupta thought there would be an 8- to 12-anna crop, and didn't see any reason to expect a famine. (The anna was a widely-used fractional measurement: there were 16 annas in the rupee, so Gupta was expecting that between half and two thirds of the crop would be saved.)

The loss of human life, Gupta explained, had been out of proportion to the crop damage. The main problem, as the paddy became ready for harvest, was the shortage of reapers. In an ordinary year the work would be done by men from neighbouring districts. But Gupta was worried that stories of the disaster would reach the labourers and stop them from making their annual migration. He asked Barton to ensure that the magistrates of Faridpur and Dacca made it known that the crops had only been partly damaged, and that the demand for reapers was greater than ever.

This was true enough for Bakarganj. But Temple had made a serious mistake in evaluating the overall prospects of the crops. Taking the part he saw for the whole, he had assumed that the damage had been uniform along the coast. On the western side of the estuary the waves had been of fresh water, but in the centre and the east they had been brackish or salty. All the crops seaward of the Chittagong trunk road had been flooded by salt water. The cultivators had been hoping for rain to wash out the salt, but it hadn't come. In a week or two the crops would wither and die. Until then they would supply fodder for the remaining cattle, but wouldn't give more than a little sustenance to the people. The crops had been coming up well, and the cultivators had been hoping to make up their losses after a run of bad harvests. But now there would be nothing. The ground was so salty that it would remain sterile until fertilised by next year's rains, and it would be another two or three years before it returned to its usual fertility.

The damage to the crops in Chittagong saw a large number of petitions made for relief. On 7 November alone the collector, John Veasey, was presented with 170 petitions, many of them signed by a number of different people. Another fifty were submitted the next day. And more direct methods of asserting a claim to relief were also attempted. When Veasey left his house for the office on 8 November he was met by about 100 cultivators and labourers asking for food, clothing, and assistance to emigrate. Veasey wasn't impressed: he told them that by assembling in a crowd, 'evidently intended to overawe', they were only hurting their own cause. Besides, he said, it was still too early to discuss questions of relief. (Out in the mofussil Veasey's thuggish deputy, J.T. Jarbo, had adopted a less diplomatic method of refusal, dispatching any cultivator who came to him for help with a few strokes of his club.)

The cultivators of Dakhin Shahbazpur and the Bakarganj mainland hadn't been affected by the salt water. But they did have other problems to deal with. Temple knew that most of the betel nut trees had been felled by the storm, and that most of the crop, which was just then being harvested, had been destroyed. What he didn't know was how important the betel nut orchards were to the local economy. Next to rice, betel nut was the district's most valuable commodity: it had a high export value, its yield was constant, and it could be sold by the cultivator when no other crop was in the ground. It was especially valuable as a fallback in years when the crop of winter rice was lean. In 1876 the winter rice would be lean indeed, and the cultivators wouldn't get anything from the sale of their betel nuts either.

The situation became much worse in Bakarganj on 23 November, just two days after Temple's minute was issued. There was another storm: people said it was the ghost of the cyclone. This time there was no wave, but the wind and rain caused great distress. Those who hadn't been able to rebuild their houses suffered terribly. 'The continual drenching in a biting wind for near 48 hours, without any shelter of any kind, is enough to freeze the blood', Gupta said.

The effect of the ghost cyclone on the crops was perhaps even worse than its predecessor. There was no layer of water to break the force of the wind, and the plants that had been saved in October were flattened. The storm also brought several days of cloudy weather. Such weather, when it came just before the harvest, provided ideal breeding conditions for black rice beetles. The beetles could strip a whole field in three or four nights. And this was what happened in 1876: the insects came out of the ground, crawled up the stalks, and finished off what the gale had begun.

The damage to the government's estates on Dakhin Shahbazpur was recorded by the deputy collector Ananda Sen. Sen found the inhabitants of char Bhuta ragged and miserable, living 'like so many persons surviving a shipwreck'. They had been hoping for a crop of 7 or 8 annas, 'a tolerably fair harvest'. But the ghost cyclone had burst the ears of unripe grain, and the insect plague had done further damage. Now they would get only 2 annas at best—an eighth of the expected crop. Sen couldn't tell whether they had any money saved, but as they hadn't managed to rebuild their homes he thought it unlikely. There were no stores of grain from previous years: the bold assertions of Temple's minute had been fantasy. Half of the population had been swept away, but the present harvest would hardly be enough to feed the survivors. There was no way for them to rebuild their houses, pay their rents, or buy clothes, plough cattle, or seeds. Many were getting ready to leave the estate. If the crop had been saved, Sen thought, they could have faced the disaster with 'firmness of mind'; but the loss of even the part left to them after the storm-wave had made them listless and depressed.

It was the same story on the other estates along the coast. Sen's notes on their condition read like epitaphs. On Jainagar: 'The ryots [cultivators] of this place ... were not in well-to-do circumstances in life, and the loss they have sustained is enough to crush them down.' On Nulgora: 'It is the poor class of men who are expected to suffer. The only hope of these men was on the outturn of the present crop, and with its failure, their hearts have also failed.'

Cultivators in the wave-affected areas also had to deal with the loss of their cattle. In many parts 80 or 90 per cent of the cattle had been drowned. Most of these had been bullocks and cows: the buffaloes were stronger and better swimmers, and more had survived. Bullocks would be needed in a few months to plough the fields for next year's crops. If they were not replaced soon the land would remain uncultivated. And there were other difficulties in preparing the land for new crops. The cultivators' stores of seed grain had been washed away or ruined, and their agricultural implements had been lost or destroyed—the roads of Chittagong district, the commissioner observed, were lined with broken ploughs.

Some cultivators, especially in Chittagong, were also having trouble rebuilding their homesteads. The government had recently imposed tolls on common building materials from the forest—thatching grass, bamboos, rattans. The commissioner, Alexander Smith, asked for the tolls to be suspended for two months to give the poorer people a chance to rebuild. But Temple refused. Such a measure, he said, would establish 'a harmful precedent'.

Perhaps the most pressing—and most dangerous—problem of all was the polluted water supply. On the eastern side of the estuary the salt water from the storm-wave had poured into the tanks, leaving the water undrinkable. Veasey tried to arrange for one of the smaller tanks in each village to be cleared out, but Smith thought this wouldn't be necessary: the people, he said, could go to the springs and hill streams for water. Regardless of whether the water in the tanks was salt, brackish, or fresh, most of them were still full of corpses and carcasses, and so foul that they could hardly be approached. Temple had been shocked at their condition. 'The streamlets which carry off the accumulated water', he noted, 'were flowing black and thick with putrid substances.' But he made no allowance for having the problem fixed.

Such an oversight was not especially surprising. Temple's tour of the affected districts had been little more than an attempt to fit what had happened into a preconceived plan. He had seen only the western side of the estuary, and had badly misjudged the effect of the storm-wave on the crops in Chittagong and much of Noakhali. His minute had been issued before the ghost cyclone of 23 November, but it seems unlikely that the effects of this storm—most importantly the loss of the remaining crops in Bakarganj—would have made much difference to his response. He had a ladder to climb.

☙

Temple's intervention brought the relief work that had been started to a swift end. In Noakhali his refusal to send a government steamer had been balanced by the Nawab of Dacca's offer of his own steamer, the *Star of Dacca*, which brought as much rice as it and two large boats could carry. But there was nothing more, and over the course of the next week the supply of relief to the affected areas was cut off completely. Nandalal Sen, on relief duty in Amirganj, was told on 14 November that no more rice was to be given and that supplies of salt and cloth were also to be stopped. Sen tried to explain that there were people on the coast still needing food, but Porch refused to listen. 'I request that you will submit a better report. I am of the opinion that relief in rice is not really needed.' Porch was especially irritated to find that Sarada Sarkar, the subdivisional officer of Feni, had tried to get the merchants there to sell their rice at a reasonable price. 'No interference with the bazar rates can be allowed', he told him. 'Rice merchants and traders should be encouraged to speculate.'

In Chittagong Veasey had already been told not to supply any more rice free of charge, and was now told not to offer any more for sale either. Local stocks in the markets were expected to be sufficient for local needs. Just as in Noakhali, there was no discussion of how a refusal to import rice or control prices might affect poorer cultivators, labourers, boatmen, and others with little money and no rice stocks of their own.

On 19 November Temple sent a special officer, Fleetwood Pellew, to Sandwip and Hatia to restore order and take any measures necessary for relief. Pellew had a reputation for being able to write excellent official reports, and was also known for his lack of sympathy for 'the natives': the right kind of man for the job. Temple knew that he would follow his orders implicitly—he hardly needed to be told that he was to 'be very economical spending money'. One of his tasks was to set up observation posts on the islands to ensure that the people were being 'thoroughly watched'. This, Temple said, was so cases of starvation could be identified—if anyone looked as though they were about to die, they would be given some food. But it was also related to another of Pellew's tasks, which was to stop any attempts at plundering and to assure people, especially outside traders, that their boats and property would be safe. The people of the islands needed watching for more reasons than one.

After receiving Temple's orders Frederick Peacock, the commissioner of Dacca, made his way to Bakarganj to supervise the shutting down of relief work there. Gratuitous relief, he said, might have been needed in Golachipa for the first few days after the storm, but it would now be stopped and grain and salt sold at cost price. The Rabnabad islands had felt the full force of the wave and lost over 70 per cent of their population, but the survivors—astonishingly—'exhibited no signs of distress', so relief would be stopped there too. H.N. Harris, the superintendent of police, was told to finish his work at Daulatkhan, sell off the remaining salt, rice, and dal, call in the other relief officers, and return to head-quarters. Peacock's attitude in all this was a distinctly punitive one. 'The people as a body seem to have behaved shamefully', he wrote. They had been taking whatever they could lay their hands on; but they wouldn't be taking any more relief. 'There is no longer any reason to suppose that the people in the tracts affected by the cyclone are in want of food, nor ... does there appear to be any necessity to adopt special measures to watch their condition', he told Temple on 19 November.

The termination of relief work was based on Temple's orders and the principles of laissez-faire rather than on any empirical data about the nature and extent of the disaster. There had been several efforts to collect statistics on the storm—losses of people, cattle, and crops, relief given and required—but these hadn't amounted to anything in practical terms. This was less because of their unreliability than their irrelevance: the decisions being made had little to do with what was actually happening on the ground. The damage to the Chittagong crops, for instance, had been known for some time, but hadn't made any difference to relief policy.

One number to come out of the statistical investigations was the number of lives lost on the night of the storm. For some time the figure quoted was 215,000. This was based on an estimate by Temple and Henry Beverley, a well-known statistician who hap-pened to be in Temple's retinue. It had been calculated, Temple explained, by determining in his presence the mortality in every house he visited, 'so as to prevent any possibility of deception', then checking this figure against the local estimates. Like many

British officials, Temple thought that the survivors and the Bengali officials had been grossly over-estimating the number of deaths. (It would later be claimed, with as little supporting evidence, that Temple's own figure was also an over-estimation.)

The lower officials had a far better understanding of the problems facing the survivors than the lieutenant governor, and found it hard to accept the decision to stop relief work. Even after Harris had been recalled to headquarters, Ananda Sen, who knew Dakhin Shahbazpur better than any other official, was still going about giving small amounts of money and grain to people along the river. There is no indication in the records of how long he was allowed to persist in this. Such activities were not looked upon kindly: the terms used to describe them, in the Victorian language of the work-house, were 'pauperisation' and 'demoralisation'.

Barton had done something similar himself in the first days after the storm, and when Temple found out about it he was not impressed. The collector's spending had amounted to Rs. 446, in sums ranging from Rs. 20 to 4 annas. Temple acknowledged that Barton had shown impressive energy in dealing with the crisis, but reprimanded him for a lack of 'care and discretion' in giving away public money. He should have given loans, not 'gifts'; and he should not do it again.

Temple sent a copy of the reprimand to Peacock, Smith, Porch, and Veasey to ensure that there would be no repeat of this behaviour. It was a humiliation for Barton: he was being criticised not only in front of his superiors, but also in front of officials of much less ability—Porch and Veasey—whose lack of initiative and humanitarian concern had kept them out of trouble. (Shortly after the letter was sent the *Indian Daily News* wrote that Barton's energy and ability 'had better not be mentioned ... as it might possibly prejudice the Bengal powers that be against one of the ablest district officers that Bengal ever had'; the paper had probably heard of the reprimand through its Bakarganj correspondent, the missionary George Kerry.)

Barton tried to justify his actions by pointing out that the disaster had been 'sudden and complete', and that there hadn't been any room for indecision. He had given the money to people who had no grain of their own and no means of buying any—carpenters, blacksmiths, other artisans. These people had arrived in Barisal from Daulatkhan bruised and wounded, near-naked, 'reduced to the extremest destitution'. They had been living for days on rotten rice and the seeds of plantains. Barton had acted according to the principle that 'they knew their own needs better than I did'. It was a principle that Temple, blinded as he was by dreams of advancement, could never have understood.

The final accounts reveal the government's pathetically small contribution to relief work after the disaster. Barton reported an expenditure of only Rs. 22,023 on what he himself called 'one of the most fearful calamities recorded in the histories of modern times'. 'Considering that the calamity overspread a population of about 700,000 souls, and was itself of a gigantic description, I hope this expenditure will be considered to be reasonable.'

The Bengalee, a Calcutta newspaper, could hardly restrain itself. 'Reasonable! We consider it to be unreasonable in the highest degree. Five times the sum would hardly have sufficed to relieve the sufferers ... we do not accuse Mr. Barton, who showed energy enough in dealing with the calamity and was as liberal as the present economic mania of Government permitted him to be; we only wonder at his apologetic tone.'

The figure from Bakarganj works out at about half an anna of relief per person: at a time when rice was selling for Rs. 5 per maund, it amounts to the one-off provision of a cup and a half of rice. The figures in the other cyclone-affected districts were far lower: only Rs. 3036 was spent in Noakhali, and about Rs. 1600 in Chittagong.

The maintenance of the government's power and influence had been at the centre of its relief plan. Temple's instructions were clear about the need to employ extra police to stop plundering, if necessary at the expense of the survivors. And in his minute he had described the relief centres as being 'as much for guard as for relief'. 'Gang robbery used to prevail formerly in these tracts,' he wrote, 'and the robber spirit still survives among the instincts of the people.' In Noakhali, the only district for which figures are available, Rs. 3253 was spent on additional police—Rs. 200 more than had been spent on relief.

CR

It is hard to tell from the official records how the zamindars of Bakarganj and Noakhali responded to the cyclone. All that is available are incidental comments in the reports of the local officers. At Gazipur, on Dakhin Shahbazpur, the relief officer Ohiduddin Mahomed asked Barton to issue the landlord with a decree to supply his tenants with food: little was evidently being done there. On Sandwip, Pellew saw that the zamindar's agents and the owners of smaller holdings were present and managing their properties, but doesn't mention whether any relief measures were being taken.

In Noakhali district as a whole, Porch reported, only the managers of estates under the government's Court of Wards had shown any concern for the victims of the storm-wave. 'The other landlords ... have not yet done anything towards giving the needy ryots any assistance in any way, though called upon to do so, nor will they attempt anything in this way unless they are compelled.' One landlord was asked to arrange for the removal of the dead bodies on his estate: he replied that he was 'praying day and night to God for the benefit of the ryots, and the country generally', but was unable to do anything else.

The government itself was one of the largest landlords in Bakarganj and Noakhali, and most of its property was in the worst-affected areas—the chars and the forest clearings. In refusing to help its own tenants it had led by example. There were also other reasons for the landlords to turn away. Many of them were engaged in bitter disputes with their tenants over rent. The Faraizis had encouraged cultivators to combine against their landlords, and a prominent landlord in Faridpur, just north of Bakarganj, had recently been murdered by his tenants. On the very day that news of the cyclone arrived, the *Soma Prakash*, a paper of Calcutta's Hindu landlords, was describing the Muslim cultivators of eastern Bengal as a 'most unquiet, selfish, and hard-hearted people'—'a source of considerable annoyance'. Such landlords must have felt a certain satisfaction in seeing their unruly tenants reduced to desperation by the storm.

The religious composition of Bakarganj also shaped the missionary response to the cyclone. At the time of the storm there were three Baptist missionaries based in Barisal—George Kerry, Thomas Martin, and their Bengali assistant John Sarkar. Although the Baptists had made more converts in Bakarganj than in any other district of Bengal, the community was still a tiny one: there were only 4000 converts out of a population of nearly two million. Nearly all of the converts had come from the low-caste Chandals, who lived in the swamps of the district's north-west; no Muslims had converted, and there were no Christians (except a few officials from other parts) in the southern subdivisions.

Martin had arrived in Barisal in March 1876 and been joined by Kerry in April. They had both worked in Bakarganj before, and were accustomed to the difficulties of missionary work in the district: holding prayer-meetings in boats or on the banks of rivers, dealing with the harassment of Christian tenants by angry zamindars, parrying the attempts of other denominations to make off with their converts. They did not lack an audience for their preaching, though this was mainly because followers of Hinduism or Islam liked to hear the other religion debunked. 'First we find fault with the Hindu gods,' one Baptist preacher explained, 'then we find fault with Mohammed, and last of all we give a little bit about Christ.' The principle was one that William Carey, the pioneering Baptist missionary and advocate of improvement, would have appreciated—'the mind of man is like a jungle; you must cut down the natural exuberant growth before you can plant it with rice'. The problem, though, was that the listeners left before the planting could begin. 'As soon as we begin to speak about Christ, the congregation disperses.'

The Baptist Missionary Society had responded energetically to the Bengal famine of 1873–74. Kerry, at that time working in Calcutta and the 24 Parganas, had been especially active in bringing the threat of famine to the Society's notice. (The 24 Parganas was second only to Bakarganj in the number of Baptist converts; as in Bakarganj, the converts were mostly poor cultivators, labourers, or boatmen.) The Society's relief appeal concentrated on the needs of the Baptist converts. Over £3000 was raised from the churches in Britain, accompanied by prayers and 'expressions of deepest sympathy'. The money was more than enough to help Hindus and Muslims as well as Christians in the affected districts. 'In no instance', the *Missionary Herald* reported afterwards, 'was relief confined to the native Christian community.'

Like many others in Barisal, Kerry and Martin sat up all night on 31 October. In the morning they found that the house of their assistant, John Sarkar, had been ruined. The house would have been the least of Sarkar's concerns—his son, a police officer, was stationed at Daulatkhan, and if there had been a storm-wave he would have been caught by it. The arrival of Deenanath Sarkar at the station on the morning of 3 November, lacerated, bruised, and half-starved after his ordeal, must have come as a great relief.

Kerry was worried about the Baptist converts in the northwest. But he knew that they wouldn't have suffered from the storm-wave, and that the storm itself would have been less violent there than in the south. So he offered his services (and the use of the mission boat) to Barton, who gave him food and money to take down to Dakhin Shahbazpur. The letters he wrote to Barton detailing his passage downriver were reprinted in Calcutta's *Indian Daily News*. So was his recommendation that the government should send relief steamers with further supplies. 'You will, I doubt not,' he added in a note to the paper, 'raise your voice to help the people.'

One of the subjects suggested for prayer by the Baptist Missionary Society was 'that the great calamity might be the means of disposing people to hear and accept the Gospel'. Similar pious hopes had been expressed during the famine of 1873–74. 'Let it be the earnest prayer of the churches', the *Missionary Herald* had written, 'that this dire calamity may lead multitudes to reflect on the follies and wretchedness of idolatry, and on the worthlessness of the gods they serve.' The charge of idolatry could hardly be levelled at the puritanical Muslims of southern Bakarganj, but the cyclone was nevertheless seen as an opportunity for evangelism. As a relief officer, Kerry, according to the *Missionary Herald*, 'had the opportunity of preaching the truth and administering the consolations of the Gospel to many thousands whom he might not otherwise have reached'. Kerry himself reported an increased interest in his preaching after the storm, but there is no evidence that any of the survivors changed their religion.

The missionaries seem to have continued their contribution to disaster relief after Kerry's journey to Dakhin Shahbazpur. Much of the Bengal famine fund remained unspent, and the Missionary Society's accounts show that around £200 (Rs. 2000) was drawn from it in 1876–77, most likely for use in Bakarganj. (In May 1877 it was stated in the *Missionary Herald* that 'whoever else may forget the cyclone of October 31st ... *we* cannot'.) But there is no mention of how the money was used, or who it was used on.

As Kerry had requested, the *Indian Daily News* made a public appeal on behalf of the victims of the storm-wave. 'Surely Sir

Richard Temple has anticipated the needs set forth by our correspondent and has sent relief', the paper wrote. 'But it may not be wise to act on the supposition that he has done all that is required ... the suggestion is that Calcutta should move at once.' The *Hindoo Patriot*'s Dacca correspondent Janokinath Roy also appealed 'to the sympathy of the generous public, that in every district meetings should be held and subscriptions raised in aid of the distressed people'. The force of his appeal was undermined, though, by the editorial views of his paper, which took the government at its word and told its readers that 'for the most part the survivors do not want charitable relief'.

In the event, Calcutta and the rest of Bengal hardly moved at all. Only Rs. 12,718 was raised from public subscriptions. Most of it was in the form of donations by prominent philanthropists. The main donor was Khajah Abdul Ghani, the Nawab of Dacca, who gave Rs. 5000; his estates in Bakarganj had escaped the wave, if not the effects of the gale. There was also a donation of Rs. 2500 by Kali Krishna Tagore of Calcutta. (Although they had never visited their properties in the district, the Tagore family were the largest landowners of Bakarganj.) The only donor with no property in the cyclone-affected areas was Maharani Swarnamoyee, the holder of the Cossimbazar estate, who gave Rs. 3000. Nothing came from the British merchants or officials of Calcutta, who this time around were firmly behind Sir Richard Temple. More surprisingly, nothing came from the Bengali middle class: they protested loudly against the government's relief policy in their newspapers, but when it came to paying for their opinions they were nowhere to be found.

There was, astonishingly, a proposal that the government should use the donations that had been received to cover its own expenses. After being told off by Temple, Barton had become as zealous as his superiors on questions of government spending. Instead of being given to the people as 'gifts', he suggested, three quarters of the subscriptions should be given as loans. The government could then collect the repayments on these loans to offset its relief spending. Peacock thought it a fine idea: it would 'go to recoup Government the expense it incurred in relieving distress immediately after the cyclone, which would, but for the great urgency of the case, have been a duty incumbent on the landowners'. But even Temple couldn't approve of this extraordinary scheme: Peacock was quietly told that 'the subscriptions should be expended, as intended by the donors, on the relief of the distressed'.

After the cyclone of 1867—which caused far less damage and far fewer deaths than the 1876 storm—Rs. 90,000 had been raised by public subscription. That sum had been matched by the government. The list of subscribers in the relief committee's report is nine pages long, and includes virtually every prominent British and Bengali resident of Calcutta. Why was so much more given in 1867 than in 1876? The horrors of the 1866 Orissa famine were then a matter of recent memory, and perhaps of conscience too; the famine of 1873–74 had left no such dreadful mark. The 1867 cyclone had affected Calcutta, the capital of British India; Bakarganj and Noakhali were isolated and unimportant districts. The victims then had been the Hindu cultivators of the western seaboard; now they were the troublesome Muslims of the east (though many low-caste Hindus suffered from the 1876 storm too). Whatever the reasons, the public's response to the cyclone of 1876 was as trifling as the government's had been.

CR

By the 1870s Bengal had a vigorous Bengali-owned press, with papers in English as well as the Bengali vernacular. These papers professed loyalty to the Crown, but were often severe in their criticisms of the government. Their reportage and commentary on the cyclone offers a useful counter-balance to the official version of events.

The first news of the disaster reached the Calcutta papers on 6 November: Peacock's telegram had arrived earlier that day from Dacca. The response from *The Bengalee*, a paper of the Bengali gentry, was one of anxiety for both the survivors of the cyclone and the residents of the metropolis. 'Backergunge is the great rice Golah [granary] of Calcutta,' it wrote, 'and any great calamity there cannot but affect us materially.' The paper thought there hadn't been such a terrible disaster in Bengal since the famine of 1770. Relief in large quantities would have to be provided by the government, the landlords, and 'fellow countrymen in affluent circumstances'—the readers of *The Bengalee*. If it wasn't forthcoming, the paper added, disease would be sure to follow.

Debate in the Bengali papers of late 1876 was dominated by two topics. One was the forthcoming imperial durbar at Delhi, at which Queen Victoria would be proclaimed empress of India. The other was the famine underway in southern and western India. The coincidence of these two events had already led the papers to question the government's financial priorities. Now the cyclone was brought onto the stage too. 'Bengal is in no mood for mirth', *The Bengalee* wrote. 'She has lost by the storm-wave of the 31st ultimo in all likelihood about several hundred thousands of her children ... The Deccan is being desolated by a widespread famine, the full magnitude of which is not yet known. And yet our rulers are about to proclaim with the sound of trumpets an addition to the royal title which no one in particular is fond of.' The great expense of the durbar was coming at a time when the government's finances were, by its own admission, not in good shape. 'In the present position of the Exchequer, it is not pleasant to think of half a million sterling being wasted on an approaching state pageant.'

The tone of the criticisms became more aggressive as it became clear that they were being ignored. In a neat inversion of the justification for the durbar—that Indians were incapable of understanding power without spectacle—*The Bengalee* described the event as a product of Disraeli's 'oriental imagination'. If it took place while the country was in the grip of a famine, and had just suffered the worst cyclone disaster in recorded history, it would leave 'a very unpleasant impression'. 'What is necessary for the Government to prove at this moment is that it thinks more of the welfare of its subjects than of personal displays of power and magnificence. The financial position of the country is such that it can hardly bear the expenses of a tamasha [grand show], while millions stand in sad need of pecuniary help.'

The vernacular papers were just as vigorous in their condemnation of the durbar. 'While thousands are spent on fireworks', the *Soma Prakash* wrote, 'thousands of men will perhaps be dying from starvation, from want of proper relief and supervision ... The English regard the people of India as a race of children fond of glitter and show. But a little reflection would prove that they have surpassed the Native Princes in this respect.' The *Bharat Mihir*, a Mymensingh weekly, thought that the viceroy, Lord Lytton, must have gone 'mad with festivities'—why else had he not shown any concern for the distress in eastern Bengal? The fiercest criticism was delivered by the *Bishwa Suhrid*, another Mymensingh paper: 'Almost everything connected with India is for the advantage of the British ... Famines, cyclones, plagues, and lamentations are all for the down-trodden natives ... The actions of Government are always, as now, attended with parade and formality; though on this occasion there is involved in them the loss of numberless human lives.'

The Bengalee used the coincidence of the durbar, the cyclone, and the famine as the starting point for a more general criticism of British rule in India. The recently issued parliamentary blue book disclosed a large trade surplus, effectively a tribute paid by India to England. 'This annual drain exhausts our resources and makes this country so poor.' Recurrent disasters were the most obvious symptoms of this structural inequality. 'Within a decade India has had four famines ... She has ceased to be a manufacturing country and she has not the wherewithal to buy food. She is wretchedly impoverished and the impoverishment is proceeding at a rapid rate.'

The British-owned papers of Calcutta took a different view of the durbar and its relation to the cyclone and famine. The *Friend of India* was the most liberal among them. 'To the future Historian of India, it will be no mean proof of the efficiency of the British administration of the country at this period, when he finds that, in spite of such fearful natural calamities as an inundation sweeping away more than 200,000 human beings in a night, and famine over-spreading a great part of the south and west of the peninsula ... the Government went calmly on its way to the celebration of perhaps the greatest State pageant in history ... while at the same time an organised system of relief was established all over the distressed tracts ... so perfect that food was more abundant in many of the stricken regions than in common years of plenty.'

The article might be read as a well-aimed satire. But its sentiments seem to have been sincere: it concludes that the British are too ready to criticise themselves and their government, and by doing so set the 'natives' a bad example.

❧

The natives' response to Temple's minute on the cyclone was as forthright as their criticism of the durbar. There had been hopes that the lieutenant governor would lead another successful relief mission: he still had a reputation for generosity, acquired during the famine of 1873–74. *Amrita Bazar Patrika*, when it learned that he was touring the affected areas, reassured its readers that 'fortunately Sir Richard Temple is there and will have the opportunity of seeing things with his own eyes'. But it soon became clear that Temple's ideas had changed. *The Bengalee* wondered whether 'a lofty position justifies what would be looked upon as signs of hard-heartedness in the low vale of life'. The instructions Temple had left with the local authorities in the cyclone-affected districts looked 'a little like callousness to human suffering'. 'Such an exhibition of a miserly disposition in so grave a crisis was quite uncalled for.' Uncalled for, perhaps, but not entirely unexpected: Temple had long been conscious that the financial aspect of any question was the first that the government considered, 'and his experiences in the famine campaign and the rough handling he met with in consequence have only served to quicken his financial susceptibilities'.

Amrita Bazar saw Temple's relief policy as just another selective and self-serving application of the principles of political economy. Advocating free trade and denouncing protection was all very well now that Indian manufacturing had been destroyed and the country turned into an agricultural colony. Temple's minute, it concluded, was the product of an exploitative mindset conditioned more by profit-hunger than principle. 'We have no words to express adequately our indignation against the action of the Government at this juncture.'

Analyses of the minute also appeared in the vernacular papers. The *Bharat Mihir* thought that the 'Black Pamphlet' had caused Temple to dramatically change his attitude to relief. He might not have directly forbidden the distribution of food, but the way he had phrased his orders was 'apt to be misconstrued and likely to cause serious mischief'. 'We are no advocates of extravagance, but are afraid that, in their eagerness to conform to this order, many an officer will withhold relief where it is really needed.' There had already been reports of officials refusing to help people in distress: in some parts of Chittagong people had come 8 miles to get food, only to return 'with half a seer of rice and with thoughts of the morrow'. The *Bishwa Suhrid* was just as critical of the minute. Temple's instructions, it thought, 'betray unmistakeably the niggardliness of his disposition, as well as a sad want of sympathy with the survivors'.

The *Friend of India* was more respectful towards the lieutenant governor, but it too had questions about the tone and substance of his minute. He had been quick to conclude that the people would be able to pay their rent and the government collect its revenue. How, it asked, could the loss of some of the revenue be avoided? Many of the taxpayers had drowned, and the survivors had lost large parts of their rice and betel nut crops. They now needed to rebuild their houses and replace their cattle. The paper wondered whether the famine of 1873–74 was actually a suitable point of comparison. Had it really been an 'infinitely greater' calamity than the cyclone? The people in the famine districts hadn't lost their cattle, their houses, or their fruit trees. There had been a good season afterwards, and relief had been plentifully distributed, 'as the Lieutenant-Governor knows'. The consequences of the cyclone were going to take much time and money to fix, but Temple was acting almost as though nothing had happened.

An exception to the widespread criticism of the government's inaction was provided by the *Hindoo Patriot*, the paper of the zamindar-dominated British Indian Association. Like the other papers, the *Patriot* at first hoped that Temple's presence would stimulate relief work; unlike the other papers, it maintained this hope in the face of all evidence to the contrary. Temple and his retinue were described as 'ministers of grace'; they had apparently given the survivors of the cyclone a sense that 'the Government was in the air, moving with them, living with them, and sympathising with them'. Temple, the paper claimed, had solved the problem of merchants combining to raise the price of rice simply by 'a feeling appeal ... on the behalf of suffering humanity'. The paper followed the lieutenant governor in underestimating the difficulties faced by the survivors, and even repeated his claim that they had large underground stocks of food. These (non-existent) stocks, it believed, would 'enable them to set up in life again'. There was a belated request that the government supply 'fuller details of relief measures'; but it was hardly enough for the *Patriot* to escape charges by its rivals, and even by its own correspondent in eastern Bengal, of culpable credulity.

It was easier for the Bengali papers to criticise the government than their own readers. *Amrita Bazar* was the only one that looked at the response of the Bengalis themselves, and it was not impressed with what it saw. 'A most calamitous visitation has overtaken the country, and the people manage to sleep over it ... not a trace of emotion is visible in all Calcutta.' At least the government officers, and even Temple, were 'up and doing'; the Bengali professional and landowning classes were simply ignoring the disaster. 'A people so enthusiastically apathetic cannot, should not prosper ... When foreigners care more for our country than we do ourselves, we have no business to speak of the country as our country.' The paper urged the public to stir themselves and 'do their duty', as the cyclone sufferers were still in urgent need of relief. Any subscriptions raised after this lapse of time (it was two months after the storm) were not going to make them comfortable, but would at least help them get started again.

On 1 January the day of the durbar arrived. *The Bengalee* professed its satisfaction in its usual sarcastic manner. 'It is an occasion for rejoicing and we would not mar the effects of it by any more reference to the thousands of unhappy wretches whose corpses lie yet unburied in Eastern Bengal or the millions who are threatened with starvation in Southern and Western India.' The celebration in Calcutta was presided over by Temple's private secretary, Charles Buckland, who tactfully desisted from his habit of referring to Her Majesty's Bengali subjects as 'niggers'.

Temple, of course, was attending the assemblage in Delhi, where he had his own camp. He was thoroughly enjoying it—the ceremonies, the receptions, the banquets. Best of all, he was back in favour with the highest authorities, who had commended him for his 'characteristic energy' in dealing with the cyclone. And that energy was about to win him further recognition. One evening at the assemblage he was taken aside by Sir John Strachey, who in 1874 had been one of his harshest critics (he had called the famine relief effort 'a vast picnic'). Strachey told him that the government was becoming anxious about the famine in southern and western India. They wanted to send a delegate to Madras, and asked whether Temple could recommend anybody. Temple recommended himself, and was accepted.

'While hundreds of thousands of human beings have lost their lives, and as many their property in Eastern Bengal, the Lieutenant-Governor has been promoted to a higher office ... He will not be missed.' This was the verdict of the *Hindu Hitoishini*, a Dacca newspaper, on Temple's departure. Of the few who had profited from the cyclone, perhaps none had profited more than Sir Richard Temple. His merciless adherence to laissez-faire had redeemed his reputation for profligacy and earned him the promotion he so desired. But it had also blinded him to the difficulties facing the survivors of the storm, and opened the way to serious long-term problems in the cyclone-affected districts.

Of more immediate concern, the government's policy had left much of the population without adequate food, water, or shelter. The tanks and fields were full of decomposing bodies. The survivors were hungry, weak, and living in filth. Conditions were perfect for the spread of disease. Cholera had already broken out in some parts, and would soon grow into an epidemic of terrible proportions.

5

THE EPIDEMIC

A narrow alluvial plain was all that separated the outer ranges of the Chittagong hills from the Bay of Bengal. On the highest of these hills, visible from well out to sea, was a large white temple. The temple was an object of pilgrimage, sacred to the gods Sati and Shiva. The ascent to it was said to release the pilgrim from the misery of a future birth. Just below it, on the slope, was a smaller temple marking the site of an old hot spring. Sita, in exile with Rama, was said to have bathed here, and the name given to the spring—Sitakund—had also been given to the hill and the small town at its base.

Every year the religious festivals of Sitakund attracted pilgrims from all over Bengal. One of the most important was Kartik purnima, marking the full moon in the Bengali month of Kartik. In 1876 the festival fell on 2 November. On the night of the cyclone there were two or three thousand pilgrims in and around the town, preparing for the celebrations. Many were staying on the coast in their boats; around a thousand of them were drowned by the wave. The town itself was badly damaged. Most of the houses on the coast side of the Dacca road, which ran through Sitakund on an embankment raised above the plain, were destroyed. The surviving pilgrims crowded into the houses left standing on the other side. And then the cholera broke out.

The first official on the scene was Frederick Pargiter, an assistant magistrate sent to Sitakund on relief duty. He found that the police had been carrying out the dead and placing them by the roadside, and ordered that the bodies be taken to the middle of the fields instead. He was worried that the disease would be spread by the pilgrims on their way home. On 6 November he advised the commissioner of Chittagong, Alexander Smith, that medical help would be needed from Dacca. 'The strength of our medical staff', he explained, 'is not sufficient to cope with an emergency of this nature.' Cholera was now 'raging ... in a most virulent form'. Two days later Pargiter himself came down with the disease.

On 5 November Reginald Porch, the collector of Noakhali, reported that cholera had broken out in that district. By 10 November he was writing that it had become 'exceedingly bad and dangerous'. Already it was getting in the way of cyclone relief work: as fast as a boat-crew could be engaged, some of its members would die or be struck down and the others seized by a panic. Hatia had been cut off from the mainland since the cyclone: the cholera was so bad that the ferry service couldn't be restarted.

On the other side of the Meghna river it seemed as though Bakarganj might have escaped this latest calamity. At the time of the lieutenant governor's visit the disease hadn't yet appeared in the district. In his minute on the cyclone Temple expressed his hope that the epidemic in Noakhali and Chittagong would soon be brought under control. 'We are prepared,' he said, 'so far as medical aid goes, for the contingency of epidemic sickness.' He did, however, prudently acknowledge that things might yet take a turn for the worse.

CR

Epidemic cholera was not unusual in the districts of eastern Bengal. The first cholera pandemic had started in Jessore, the district just to the west of Bakarganj, in 1817. From Jessore the disease had spread to Calcutta; from Calcutta it had travelled up the valley of the Ganges and across central India, attacking the East India Company's army on the way. Eventually it had reached Europe.

Before 1817 cholera had been endemic, in a mild form, in nearly every district of Bengal. But the variety that emerged that year was stronger and more frightening than its predecessor. A victim of the disease, feeling hot in the stomach, would suffer a sudden collapse. The collapse would be followed by the vomiting and diarrhoea of a watery, whey-coloured liquid. There would be burning pains in the abdomen and a cold sweat. The victim would be desperately thirsty: eyes congested and sunken, voice broken, skin cold, blue, and clammy. There would be a period of restlessness, with the heart fluttering and the breathing getting slower. The diarrhoea and vomiting might begin again, but only for a time. The intervals between breaths would become longer and longer; and then there would be death.

There was a bewildering variety of theories on the cause and transmission of cholera. 'In no disease', one authority on the subject wrote, 'has there been such a diversity of opinion.' At the time of the 1876 epidemic the main point of dispute was whether it could be passed from person to person. On one side were the contagionists, whose position was consistent with the germ theory of disease. The contagionists pointed to the many instances in which cholera had appeared after the arrival of people from places where it was known to be flourishing: troops on the march from a cholera-struck camp, pilgrims dispersing from a festival. There was also evidence that contact with the diarrhoea of cholera victims, or with articles of clothing and bedding contaminated by it, had been followed by attacks of the disease.

On the other side were the anti-contagionists, who generally subscribed to some form of miasma theory. The origins of the disease, they thought, were in poisonous vapours given off by the soil or rotting vegetation. This was the view of the government of India's chief advisor on epidemic cholera, James Bryden, and of its sanitary commissioner, J.M. Cuningham. It was the anti-contagionists who had the most influence over cholera policy, partly because their position didn't require unpopular quarantine measures and expensive improvements to water supplies.

There were also those who were inclined to accept both positions. Among them was the sanitary commissioner of Bengal, John Coates. Cholera could arise spontaneously, Coates thought, but it could also be communicated from person to person. 'That cholera evacuations, whether in clothes, soil, water, food, &c., do become virulent, and do, especially when taken into the system by the mouth, give rise to cholera, I have no manner of doubt.'

Despite the different opinions on the disease's transmission, there was a consensus among medical men that its emergence was encouraged by malnutrition and poor sanitation. 'There can be little doubt', one surgeon wrote, 'that in a country like Bengal, where large bodies of the people are in a chronic state of extreme poverty, but little above starvation point, any general rise in prices must mean extreme suffering and a greatly diminished power of resisting disease.' 'It is allowed by all', another surgeon said, 'that defects in the purity of the air and water, overcrowding, improper food or clothing, and bad conservancy ... predispose to the action of the cholera poison.' In the aftermath of the cyclone all of these conditions were present, and in the most extreme form imaginable.

A further predisposing cause of the 1876–77 epidemic must have been the great number of corpses and carcasses left lying about after the storm-wave. A week after the storm a deputy collector at Bauphal, Jadunath Chowdhury, wrote of the urgent need to get bodies out of the rivers, tanks, creeks, and home-steads if cholera was to be prevented. But many of the survivors refused to handle the victims' corpses. 'The people will do nothing to remove the dead bodies,' the Baptist missionary George Kerry noted, 'and, as they are scattered over an immense area, a pestilence seems likely with starvation to complete what the storm left undone.' In Chittagong the bodies of the drowned, preserved by salt water, lay on the fields for weeks. 'In very many instances', a correspondent for the *Bengal Times* wrote towards the end of December, 'the bodies are still perfect, with every feature recognisable.'

As the epidemic went on the bodies of the cholera victims joined them. It was a nightmarish scene. 'Some dead, others dying, others just attacked ... carcasses interspersed with human corpses ... cesspools of green abominations ... the whole atmosphere heavily laden as it were with infection.' The smell of decomposition became so strong that travellers passing along the roads had to keep their noses and mouths covered; some started running when they reached a cholera-struck village and didn't stop until they had left it well behind.

Religious and caste prejudices made the situation worse. On the coast just north of Chittagong town, in a mainly Muslim area, an official found a number of Hindu corpses that he thought had floated across from Sandwip or Badu. The local Muslims wouldn't touch them, although there were many fresh Muslim graves. Even within the Muslim population—a majority in all of the districts affected by the cyclone—there were similar scruples about the disposal of bodies. Islam was supposed to be free of caste distinctions, but in practice the Muslims of the Bengal delta were divided into various exclusive sub-groups, usually based on occupation. Members of different caste groups didn't intermarry or eat together, and they certainly wouldn't touch the bodies of unidentified cyclone victims.

In Daulatkhan the superintendent of police, H.N. Harris, couldn't find anyone willing to drag the bodies out of the tanks and throw them into the creek. He had brought five Chamars— members of the untouchable sweeper caste—with him from Barisal, and ordered them to do it. The Chamars removed the cattle carcasses, but wouldn't touch the corpses. Harris sent the police to conscript some Bhumalies, a caste of even lower standing than the Chamars. Only two could be found: it wasn't nearly enough.

There were also practical difficulties in the disposal of bodies after the cyclone. The usual scavengers—jackals, dogs, vultures, crows—had disappeared. In some places the pattern of the tides meant that bodies thrown into the creek at the ebb would float back again on the flood. In other places there were too few survivors to remove the corpses; and where there were enough people, there were not enough digging tools. Together with the weakened condition of the population and the government's refusal to supply relief, the failure to dispose of the bodies created an environment in which disease could flourish.

ॐ

The government's immediate response to the outbreak of cholera in Sitakund was to send out the available 'native doctors'. These were the medical equivalent of the Indian deputies who filled the lower ranks of the civil administration. The medical service, like the civil service, was virtually closed to Indians, but Indian subordinates were still needed to carry out basic duties. After being trained in Western medicine at Calcutta Medical College these doctors usually took up positions as sub-assistant surgeons, vaccinators, or dispensary attendants; others worked for zamindars or went into private practice in Calcutta or the mofussil.

There were only two or three native doctors in government service in Chittagong. After they had been sent to Sitakund all that could be done for the rest of the district was to have the police dispense 'cholera pills'—a pleasant but ineffectual combination of essential oils, herbs, spices, and opium. On 19 November the disease broke out to the west of the town, and by 8 December it had crossed the Karnaphuli river. By the end of December it had reached as far south as Kutubdia island.

John Coates, the sanitary commissioner of Bengal, arrived in Chittagong in mid-December. After inspecting some of the cholera-struck villages he came up with a plan for making the most of the limited medical supplies at his disposal. The affected areas in Noakhali and Chittagong were divided into circles. Each circle was placed under the charge of an assistant surgeon. The government doctors (there were now nine in Chittagong) were posted to the worst-affected places to set up medical centres. Educated or influential villagers were supplied with medicines for people who lived far away from the centres, and a list of sanitary rules was prepared to be circulated as widely as possible.

Coates had originally planned to supervise the government doctors himself. But this wouldn't be possible unless he was able to get from place to place efficiently. An ordinary boat, dependent on the tides, was almost useless. So he asked for a steamer, which he proposed to use as a floating control centre, carrying medicines and personnel from place to place. Temple knew from his own experience the advantages of steamer travel in the delta. But he had refused to sanction one for food relief, and now he refused to sanction one for medical relief too.

His refusal was yet another demonstration of the government's unwillingness to spend money on disaster relief. But it also reflected a deeper ambivalence about the state's responsibility for public health. The post of sanitary commissioner had been established only in the 1860s, mainly in response to concerns about the health of the army. The commissioner had no executive powers, and a lack of financial and political support limited his effectiveness. The situation became even worse after 1870, when the central government passed the responsibility for public health to provincial administrations that were often unable or unwilling to meet even the most basic needs.

In Noakhali the disease had appeared across a greater area than in Chittagong and was spreading more rapidly. At first the only medical relief available was at the charitable hospital and dispensary in Sudharam. Every district had one of these institutions, which were paid for by a combination of government money and private subscriptions. Most of the expenses of the Noakhali hospital were met by the district's largest landowners, the raja of Bhulua and the Courjon family. The facilities were primitive: there was no separate ward for patients suffering from infectious diseases, and no female ward either. Unsurprisingly, only one out of every thirty patients stayed in the hospital itself. The rest collected their medicines from the dispensary and left. In the early stages of the epidemic, at least, there was a great demand for medicines: over a hundred people a day came to collect them for their friends and relatives. But for most people in the district, the dispensary, if they knew of it—and if they wanted Western medicine—was too far away to be of any help.

On 5 November Porch received a list of recommendations from Dr Lyons, the district's medical officer, for preventing the spread of disease in and around the town. The recommendations were tailored to cover the possibilities of both miasma and contagion. Several of them might have considerably improved the situation. The big tank in the station was to be guarded and preserved strictly for drinking supply; wells or tanks were to be excavated for drinking water in the villages to the south of the town; the latrines in the bazaar were to be cleaned up. People were to be careful about drinking water, boiling it before use. Friends or relatives of those who had the disease were to bury their diarrhoeal evacuations as soon as possible; the cholera dead were to be burnt or buried, not sunk in the creeks. But other suggestions—starting fires windward of affected villages, removing fallen trees and branches from tanks and water-courses, cutting the station's thatching-grass fields—were offered with the miasma theory in mind, and wouldn't have made much difference.

Porch had most of the recommendations concerning the town carried out. But he refused to have wells and tanks dug in the villages. This, he said, wasn't the government's responsibility—even when the villages were on government-owned land. It wasn't until Temple's arrival on 7 November that anything was done to address the outbreak of disease in the mofussil. On that day a doctor was dispatched to Sandwip, and Temple also telegraphed (via Comilla) for another four doctors to be sent to the district. Two arrived on the *Star of Dacca* on 12 November and were sent to Hatia and Sandwip. The remaining two didn't turn up for another fortnight. By then Smith had asked for four more doctors, and by 11 December they too had arrived. A few days later two assistant surgeons arrived and were placed in charge of the district's two medical circles, one covering the mainland, the other the islands.

It was around this time that Porch decided to leave Noakhali on what he later called a 'cold-weather tour'—though unlike the ordinary annual tour of the district, this one included a trip to Calcutta over the Christmas holidays. It was a jaunt (or attempt at self-preservation) that nearly cost him his job. The new lieutenant governor, Ashley Eden, took over from Temple on 8 January. A few days later he wrote to the new commissioner of Chittagong, Edmond Lowis, for information on the epidemic. 'Can anything be done to check cholera?', he asked. 'Is the magistrate showing proper activity? Keep me constantly informed of the state of public health.' But Lowis had heard nothing about the epidemic in Noakhali for more than a month. At the beginning of December he had asked Porch to submit a full report on the effects of the cyclone in Noakhali, including information on places struck by cholera; but at the time of the lieutenant governor's request the report still hadn't arrived. Lowis had to tell Eden that Porch was gone and that he couldn't tell him anything about the state of public health in Noakhali.

'Dear Porch', Lowis wrote angrily. 'I have not yet been informed of your return to the district, and I am entirely in the dark as to what steps you have taken to check the spread of cholera ... You were very foolish to run off to Calcutta.' Eden was also unimpressed, and demanded an explanation. Porch's absence from the district, at the very time the epidemic was at its peak, had led to a complete breakdown in communications between Noakhali, Chittagong, and the government in Calcutta. Why had he left when his presence was so urgently needed?

Porch was flustered: 'a proper account can be given of everything everywhere', he said. He had wanted to go to Calcutta to see his wife off on the P&O steamer; when Temple was in Noakhali he had given him verbal permission to do so. (It turned out that Lowis had also given his permission: 'Smith did not tell me anything about your going away to Calcutta, but if you got permission from the Lieutenant Governor it is alright.') The failure to recognise that a district officer needed to be in his district during a major disaster didn't reflect well on Temple or Lowis. But in the end it was Porch's mistake, and Porch who would be censured. 'In leaving his district when he did,' Eden wrote, 'in the throes of a great calamity, Mr. Porch has shown that he is wanting in that sense of duty and ability to subordinate his personal interests to the requirements of public life, which are essential to the proper administration of a district.' The question now was whether he ought to be left in charge at Noakhali.

CR

There wasn't much that could be done to treat cholera once it had taken hold, although all sorts of remedies were suggested by the various authorities. A list of medicines requested by Lyons gives an idea of the variety of the nineteenth-century cholera pharmacopoeia: 'Please order despatch of common carb 6 pounds, calomel 5 pounds, camphor 10 pounds, cajeput oil ½ pound, chlorodyne 6 pounds, chloroform 2 pounds, cantharides powder 2 pounds, ipecac powder 3 pounds, mustard 50 pounds, nitric ether 10 pounds, opium 1 pound, peppermint oil ½ pound, liquor lyttoe 6 pounds, rectified spirit 9 pounds, soda 10 pounds, sulphate ammonia aromat 5 pounds, sulphuric acid 5 pounds, tincture cardamom 5 pounds.'

The medicines could be given either as pills or as liquids. Pills didn't offend caste prejudices about handling liquids, and were generally thought to be superior. But during the 1876 epidemic they were rejected in favour of drinkable medicines. 'If the native doctors have nothing but cholera pills to distribute,' Coates wrote, 'they may as well be withdrawn; for the people will not go the length of their houses to have pills dispensed to them, though they gladly accept, and come considerable distances for chlorodyne or cholera mixture.' There was no explanation of why this might be, and it didn't really matter: neither the pills nor the liquid were any use.

The failure of the government doctors to treat the disease gave the supporters of homeopathy a chance to advertise their own system. The merits of allopathy and homeopathy were the subject of much debate among Bengali physicians, especially after the conversion to homeopathy of Mahendralal Sarkar, a leading physician trained at Calcutta Medical College. The *Bharat Sangskarak*, commenting on the loss of life from cholera in Chittagong, thought that 'the almost incredible number of deaths undeniably proves that the allopathic treatment of this disease is almost useless. We have a firm conviction that, under homeopathic treatment, better results would undoubtedly follow.' The paper asked the government to appoint a commission made up of both allopathic and homeopathic doctors to inquire into the matter. What it didn't mention was that the recommended homeopathic treatment for cholera, strong tincture of camphor—a remedy that didn't even follow the homeopathic principle of 'like curing like' or the homeopathic technique of extreme dilution—was already among the many potions in the government doctors' medical chests.

Even if the government doctors had been able to treat the disease, there were not nearly enough of them to attend to all its victims. And even if there had been enough, many cholera patients would still have chosen, as they did in cases of ordinary illness, to consult a practitioner of Indian medicine. In Bengal the practice of Ayurveda was closely linked to the Baidya caste, which after the establishment of the Calcutta Medical College also supplied many of the doctors trained in Western medicine. There were a number of Baidyas in the north of Bakarganj, and the district was well known for its Ayurvedic practitioners. There were also practitioners of Yunani medicine. But in the south of Bakarganj and in Noakhali it was more likely that a person suffering from the disease would have sought out the village mullah, who made much of his money from prescribing amulets (and was hostile to genuine physicians). Others might have used folk medicine, which was often administered by a low-caste barber or fisherman.

The practitioners of Indian medicine are invisible in the 1876 records, and generally ignored in the mid-nineteenth century treatises on cholera. But they appear briefly in earlier British sources. According to Jameson's report on the 1817 epidemic, their standard treatment was opium, cardamom, and chilli. Preparations of lime, decoctions of neem bark, and other astringents were sometimes used; patients were given drinks of rosewater and lemonade, rubbed with sandal-wood dust, and fanned. These methods compare favourably with the standard British techniques of the time, blood-letting and purging, both of which only killed the patient quicker. And when the British abandoned the 'heroic' methods of cholera treatment in the mid-nineteenth century they fell back on cholera pills and mixtures based on the formula of opium and spices developed by the Indian physicians.

There was probably little difference between the treatment offered by the government doctors and by the other practitioners. All measures were equally unavailing. In 1817 people showed what they thought of the human help available to them by turning to their deities. Again, there is no evidence in the official sources of popular religious responses to the 1876 epidemic. In such situations the goddess Kali could be invoked: Henry Beveridge's history of Bakarganj mentions with disapproval the behaviour of a Mr Sturt, the collector of the district in the early 1840s, who had the Kali puja celebrated in the bazaar as a means of averting the cholera. There was also a goddess of cholera, Oladevi, worshipped by Hindus as Ola Chandi and by Muslims as Ola Bibi. During cholera epidemics worship of the goddess was led by the village headmen. The puritanical Faraizis, who were especially strong in southern Bakarganj and Noakhali, had done their best to suppress the folk religion of the delta; but it would not have been surprising if the horrors of the 1876 epidemic brought the old beliefs back to the surface.

℞

Ebenezer Barton, the district officer of Bakarganj, had responded quickly to the storm-wave in the south of the district, sending out relief officers with supplies of food and money. He had also hired four doctors from Barisal and sent them out with supplies of medicine. There were countless cases of fractures, wounds, and bowel complaints for the doctors to attend to, as well as a few mild cases of cholera.

While Temple was in Bakarganj he and Barton discussed the possibility of an epidemic breaking out in the wave-affected areas, as it had already done in Chittagong and Noakhali. It was decided that two more doctors should be brought down from Dacca in readiness. The days went by, and still there was no sign of the disease in its epidemic form. Lewis Cameron, the civil surgeon, thought that the doctors from Dacca should be returned. Barton was sure that the cholera would come eventually, and asked him to keep them. But Cameron insisted on sending them back; and at the end of November he also recalled the four doctors already at work in the mofussil.

It was a bad mistake. Even if the doctors were not treating cases of cholera—and there wasn't much they could do in this regard—they were still playing an important role in improving sanitary conditions and treating other complaints. As it happened, the disease broke out shortly after they were recalled. It began at Gazipur, in the north of Dakhin Shahbazpur. By early January it had reached the south of the island. After presiding over the durbar celebrations in Bakarganj on 1 January, Barton asked the authorities in Calcutta for more doctors. But it was too late for them to make any difference. For the first ten days of January the disease raged all over the subdivision; by the end of the month it had killed nearly 8000 people.

On 7 January Cameron left Barisal on a tour of inspection of Dakhin Shahbazpur. He found the island in a state of social breakdown. 'The people are much alarmed. They have given up all their occupations, thinking that they will all sooner or later be attacked with cholera and die.' Not only had large numbers been attacked by the disease, but the mortality rate was much higher than usual (a later estimate put it at 87 per cent). Many of the island's traders had left, and cultivators who could afford it or who had relatives beyond the disaster zone had also gone. The villages on the banks of the Meghna were deserted; in villages further inland there were sometimes only five or six people to be found. In the south there were not even enough people left to bury the victims of the disease, who lay decomposing in the houses they had died in.

When Cameron returned to Barisal on 18 January he found that medical reinforcements had arrived. There was a European surgeon, Arthur Tomes, from Calcutta, an assistant surgeon, Kalidas Mookerjee, from Dacca, and five government doctors from Calcutta. Mookerjee and the doctors were sent to the south of the district. Cameron now recognised the need for systematic medical relief: it had taken a long time. He mapped out the affected areas into circles and asked for another fifteen doctors to staff them. Leaving Tomes to manage things in Barisal, he set off to inspect Patuakhali subdivision, where the disease had also now broken out.

Cameron went from Golachipa into the interior. It was a slow journey through the narrow creeks; often he had to wait until the tide rose high enough to take the boat onwards. At one village he met the zamindar Anthony D'Silva, a descendant of the Portuguese traders who arrived in Bakarganj in the eighteenth century. D'Silva told him that more than half of the inhabitants of the village had died in the storm-wave, and the rest were now in the grip of the epidemic. Cameron went for a walk through the village. The tanks were still filled with debris from the cyclone and storm-wave; only a few of the houses had been rebuilt. The air was foul with the smell of decomposing corpses, and the surfaces were covered by crawling flies. The silence was eerie. 'I saw few people on the bank', he reported. 'The baris [homesteads] appeared to be deserted.'

The official position in the weeks after the cyclone had been that Bakarganj had made an acceptable recovery and wouldn't be needing any more relief. Cameron's tours of Dakhin Shahbazpur and Patuakhali showed that that had been a fantasy. But neither Cameron nor Barton would admit that the government's relief measures had been inadequate. Instead they placed the blame for the appalling conditions on the zamindars and their agents, perhaps forgetting that the government itself was one of the largest zamindars in the district. They also blamed the survivors of the cyclone, whose 'apathy and indolence' had brought down the epidemic. Instead of further relief, Cameron proposed that extra police be brought in 'to cause the people to better themselves'.

ॐ

No place suffered more from the epidemic than Sandwip. On 19 November Temple had sent a special officer, Fleetwood Pellew, to the island to take charge of relief work. A huge shark was patrolling the island's southern tip: the cyclone had been good for sharks. The island looked as though it had been set on fire. Pellew found the people, even the most well off among them, still wearing the same mud-stained rags they had been on the night of the storm. Their makeshift shelters—parts of roofs dragged out from the trees, propped up with sticks and mud— were also serving as granaries and cholera hospitals. The paddy harvest had been interrupted: not only was the labour of the sick unavailable, but the healthy were too busy looking after them to go out to the fields. The island was littered with corpses, 'tainting the air and hideous to look upon'. Pellew arranged for them to be removed by some Chamars, several of whom caught the disease and died too.

Sandwip had had hardly any help after the cyclone. The police diaries showed that cases of cholera had been reported since the diaries were reopened on 6 November. The distribution of pills and other medicines had begun on 13 November, with the arrival of the doctor from Sudharam. When Pellew arrived there was still only a single doctor for the whole island. Even Pellew recognised that this was 'quite insufficient'. The disease was showing no signs of abating, and deaths from cholera were threatening to exceed deaths from the storm-wave. Pellew asked for nine doctors, an assistant surgeon, and a supply of cholera mixture to be sent to the island. But it was too late to make any difference.

Pellew knew that the terrible conditions after the storm had played a large part in the outbreak of the disease. 'The shock of the calamity, the depression inevitably following such prolonged and overstraining excitement, the subsequent exposure and privations of the people with their houses destroyed, their clothes blown away, their water and rice spoiled by the salt inundation, which had yet melted and carried away all their salt; all this is quite sufficient to account for the outbreak.' What he would not admit was that the government had done nothing to improve those conditions. The storm of 23 November, he claimed, had arrived before any relief measures could be taken.

There had, of course, been an opportunity to offer relief to the island, but it had been firmly rejected by Temple, and Porch had been only too happy to follow him. Now Pellew, against the evidence of his own eyes and ears, had to vindicate that decision. He had, in effect, been sent out to confirm Temple's fantasy that the island would make a satisfactory recovery without government help. It was one of the paradoxes of the free-market response to disaster: a relief officer whose job was to prove that there was no need for relief.

Pellew did his job. The signs that trade was recovering, he decided, were sufficient proof that relief was not necessary. The rice and salt he had brought with him would be sold, not given away. He had to get Umakanta Das, a deputy magistrate, to explain to some men 'what I found it rather difficult to make them understand'—that rice would only be given to people who looked as though they were about to die of starvation. 'Their tendency to ask for help', Pellew conceded, 'can do no harm as long as they have no rice.' Lowis was relieved to hear that no money would have to be spent. 'It is clear that no relief will be required. The only enemy to be contended against is disease.'

Most officials didn't see, or didn't want to see, the connection between adequate food, water, and shelter on the one hand, and susceptibility to disease on the other. The government's response to the cyclone and storm-wave had been so inadequate that the connection was perhaps not politic to make. The two calamities had to be seen separately. If they were seen together, as they were by Pellew, it had to be emphasised either that the government could have done nothing to improve the situation, or that it had done all it could in the circumstances.

Efforts to obscure the government's share of responsibility for the epidemic would be more effective if that responsibility could be placed elsewhere. Like Cameron, Pellew blamed the people of Sandwip for their situation. Many were in a state of shock after suffering the combined effects of the storm-wave and the cholera. Pellew was upset by the lack of enterprise they were showing. 'It is extremely painful to observe the effects of this depression in labourers refusing to work, and roofless householders neglecting to rebuild their homes.' They were depressed, he thought, because they had become used to a life of luxury— 'their previous prosperity is notorious and evident'. Now that they were a little less comfortable, they were unable to keep their spirits up. There were, he admitted, some people who had never been well off, but 'the poorer classes do not suffer so much in proportion as the higher classes'. In his view, immunity to disease was largely a question of pluck. 'Recovering spirits will, I believe, prove the best enemy to cholera.'

⟶⟵

By early December 1876 the epidemic had come to the attention of the Bengali press. The papers were uniformly critical of the government's half-hearted response to the outbreak of disease, which they saw as an extension of its half-hearted response to the cyclone itself. The *Bharat Mihir*, in an article criticising Temple's cyclone relief policy—'we wish that the relief granted were not so scanty as at present'—also called on the government to send more doctors and medicines to Chittagong. 'The medical aid available is not sufficient for the requirements of the district.'

Even the *Hindoo Patriot*, which had been taken in by Temple's minute on the cyclone, was no longer content to regurgitate the official version of events. 'We want facts and not general remarks', it wrote after seeing the lieutenant governor's account of the epidemic in Sandwip. 'We wish to know how many doctors have been sent, who are they, how have they been posted, on what system are they working ... are they giving medicines only or providing nourishment, is there good drinking water in those villages, if not, what means have been taken to supply it, &c?' A month earlier the paper had claimed that the government was prepared for an epidemic 'to the best of its ability', but it was now wondering whether that had been an accurate assessment. 'Has the Government done all that it could do and should have done? Could not this have been prevented to some extent?'

Some papers went further, not only pointing out the lack of medical aid, but also connecting the severity of the epidemic with the lack of relief in the weeks following the cyclone. The most perceptive analysis of the government's activities, or the lack of them, was in the pages of *Amrita Bazar Patrika*. The paper thought it was the government's failure to provide adequate food, shelter, and clothing to the cyclone's victims that had made the epidemic as deadly as it had been. 'It is a fact, and let him deny it who can, that many are perishing in the devastated districts, though not actually from starvation, but fever, and cholera &c. &c. brought on by cold, exposure, and hunger.'

It was not only official indifference that came under the scrutiny of the vernacular papers. The *Bharat Sangskarak* noted that the public had not shown much interest in helping the victims either. 'Those of the unfortunate people who were left almost half-dead by the floods are now, after suffering extreme misery, dying of disease, uncared for by Government, and unaided by the public.' And *Amrita Bazar* called on its readers, the Bengali middle class—in vain, as it turned out—to come to the aid of the sufferers, who had been left without any resources of their own. (The only example in the records of a public contribution to medical relief is that of the Barisal People's Association, which sent a deputation to Barton with Rs. 100 worth of sago and arrowroot for distribution among the sick; it also proposed to call a meeting and raise subscriptions for the disposal of dead bodies.)

The epidemic gave the Bengali papers another chance to contrast the government's extravagant spending on the durbar with its parsimony in supplying relief to the victims of the storm-wave and epidemic. *Amrita Bazar*, reporting the outbreak of the disease on Dakhin Shahbazpur, thought that 'if even a portion of the sum, raised for the purpose of a minor durbar at Calcutta, had been expended on relief operations in Eastern Bengal, an immense amount of misery might have been prevented'. The *Bharat Sangskarak* asked how, when thousands were dying of disease, 'without adopting means in the first instance to relieve their sufferings, Government could, in this untoward time, expend lakhs of rupees on fire-works and idle festivities'. It was a question that would remain unanswered.

CR

The epidemic ran on in Chittagong and Noakhali until the beginning of April 1877. The number of deaths in Chittagong was officially estimated at 14,788, nearly 3000 of which had been in Sitakund. The real figure was probably twice as high: the information supplied by the police and village watchmen was extremely patchy. In Noakhali there had been 47,783 deaths, nearly 12,000 of them on Sandwip. Porch (who had escaped demotion after his unauthorised holiday) was still expecting more to be reported, and the figure didn't include those who usually lived outside the district. Even so, Eden wrote after seeing the report, this was 'a mortality unprecedented even in the annals of cholera'. The government's contribution to reducing that mortality had been negligible: in Noakhali (the only district for which figures are available) only Rs. 739 was spent on medical relief, as against Rs. 3252 on the appointment of extra police.

There were two sets of mortality figures from Bakarganj. One was based on reports made by the village watchmen. According to these reports, there had been 10,088 deaths from cholera in Dakhin Shahbazpur and 1788 in Patuakhali. Nobody considered these figures to be very reliable. Barton thought that even at the best of times the watchmen—'these utterly illiterate and unintelligent men'—couldn't be trusted. And the cyclone had thrown the village watch system into disarray: some of the watchmen had drowned, some had died of cholera, and many of the rest hadn't turned up at the police station during the epidemic.

The other set of estimates was based on the observations of the government doctors. It gave a higher figure of 2900 for Patuakhali, but for Dakhin Shahbazpur it gave only 8000. The subdivisional officers thought that the actual figures were probably much higher. These estimates were preferred by the authorities, though again they were not especially reliable: there must have been thousands of unrecorded deaths in the outlying villages not visited by the government doctors.

The official estimate, then, was that a total of 75,000 people had died in the epidemic. The actual figure would have been above 100,000. Curiously, around this time the estimate of deaths from the storm-wave was revised downwards from 215,000 to 100,000. This was not a result of a proper census, but only of a new set of estimates by district officials. The revised figure must be in serious doubt: some of these officials were thought to have underestimated the number of deaths in the first place. For official purposes, though, it served to diminish the significance of the massive cholera mortality. Deaths from the epidemic could now be included in a total figure that was less than Temple and Beverley's original estimate of deaths from drowning alone. It even gave the impression that the government had somehow reversed the terrible effects of the storm-wave through its diligent response to the epidemic. Before the epidemic there had been 215,000 deaths on the books; afterwards— by a stroke of the pen—only 175,000.

The divisional commissioners were confident that the government had done its duty. Peacock did at least accept that the outbreak had been worsened by the conditions in which the people were living. 'It can hardly be a matter for surprise that cholera should rage among people living in an atmosphere so polluted as to be almost unbearable, especially when, in addition to this, they were insufficiently clad, indifferently housed, and badly fed.' But in these unfavourable circumstances, he thought, everything that could be done had been done. 'All possible endeavours were used to bring medical assistance as speedily and as close to the sufferers as possible.' Lowis went so far as to claim that the disease had been 'checked and successfully combated'—a statement that the families of the 60,000 dead in Chittagong and Noakhali might have been surprised to hear. Both commissioners drew attention to their preventive efforts. Before and after the outbreak, they said, they had tried to get the people to clean up their surroundings. If these efforts had failed, the apathy of the people and the lack of help from the zamindars was to blame.

Neither commissioner made the connection between the inadequacy of the government's response to the cyclone and the terrible proportions of the epidemic. The people of the cyclone-affected areas had been denied food, water, and shelter in the service of free-market theory and Sir Richard Temple's career. The policy had been carried on even after the epidemic had begun, and despite the knowledge that cholera spread especially quickly in a population weakened by hunger. The available treatment might have been ineffective, but a better-resourced sanitary intervention would have saved many lives. The officials involved in medical relief sometimes expressed doubts about the adequacy of the government's response, but these never came before the eyes of the higher authorities, let alone the public. It was left to the Bengali-language newspapers to point out the fatal connection between official indifference and the worst cholera epidemic Bengal had ever seen.

6

THE AFTERMATH

1877 had started badly for the inhabitants of the cyclone-affected districts, and there were further hardships on the way. 'The present outlook here is very dark', the Bakarganj correspondent for the *Indian Daily News* wrote (probably the missionary George Kerry). 'The troubles which have come and are coming were seen and foretold by some; but the Bengal government seems to have shut its eyes and closed its ears to all that was not pleasant, and that would seem to stand in the way of the great holiday-making at Delhi. Pestilence and famine are not got rid of by ignoring the signs of their approach, nor by writing cheerful reports.'

One of the most pressing questions was how the cultivators would recover from a poor harvest and the loss of their plough cattle. Much depended on the attitude of the zamindars, whose power over their subjects was now greater than ever. For some of them the cyclone seemed to have come as an act of providence. Cultivators who had lost everything to the storm-wave were no longer in a strong position to resist the demands of their landlords—and the landlords knew it. 'I look upon this', one zamindar said, 'as the way in which the Almighty ... has exercised vengeance upon the Government and the ryots for having combined together to torture and torment us.'

The cyclone came in the middle of a long-running rent dispute at the raja of Hill Tippera's estate in Noakhali. The raja was trying to increase the rents, and the tenants had formed an association to resist the changes. The raja had told his agents to enforce the new settlement by any means necessary. Porch was worried that the disaffected tenants might become violent, and sent a special police force to keep the raja's collecting staff from being overpowered. The charge for maintaining the police was placed on the tenants.

The tenants suffered badly from the cyclone and storm-wave, and the police asked the raja's agents to supply them with food and fresh water. But the agents wouldn't do anything without orders from the raja. And no orders came: the raja was in no hurry to help those who had so recently set themselves up against him. Porch wrote to the British political agent of Hill Tippera asking him to get the raja to send relief. 'It was expected that the Rajah would, of his own accord, have arranged to help the poor & distressed ryots of his zemindary in this District and that it would be unnecessary to send any reminder on this subject.' Coming from Porch, this wasn't especially convincing; and just a few days later he was sanctioning the retention of the special police, still at the tenants' expense, for another year.

The tenants' resistance to the rent increases didn't collapse immediately. But the balance of power had shifted. Instead of being threatened by the tenants, the raja's agents were now, if only by coercion, getting them to submit to the settlement and pay their arrears. Porch knew that the contest was nearly over, but didn't want to take the pressure off yet. 'The impoverishment of the tenantry by the cyclone & inundation makes it harder for the ryots to defray the expenses of the Special Force, but as these adversities have not affected their spirit, or broken up their combination, or lessened their disaffection, it does not seem to be a reason for releasing them.' By June 1877 the tenants had been starved out. 'The difficulty of procuring food', Porch told the superintendent of police, 'has led to the cessation of the dispute between the Rajah and his tenants.'

Peace had been restored; the raja had increased his rents; the government had ensured the security of its revenue. In order that things should stay this way a new police outpost was established on the estate. Disaster, once again, worked in favour of those who already held power and against those who didn't.

The loans given by the government after the cyclone also tended to strengthen the landlords' position. Not only were the zamindars the guarantors of the government's land revenue, but along with the superior tenure-holders they were the only people who could offer adequate security for a loan. Temple had sanctioned advances to cultivators to replace their plough cattle, but these were only to be given to tenants on government estates.

On Sandwip, for instance, a few cultivators on the government's lands were given loans at ordinary rates of interest. But those living on privately owned estates were left to raise the money they needed in the bazaar. Fleetwood Pellew, the special relief officer on the island, thought that the cultivators would 'easily' be able to repay the debts they had incurred in purchasing cattle, ploughs, seed grain, and housing materials. He knew, though, that the local moneylenders and traders would be demanding very high rates.

Even on government estates, advances usually went to the superior tenure-holders rather than the actual cultivators. On Manpura, Azmat Ulla was loaned Rs. 1000 to bring new cultivators to the island and keep it from 'relapsing into jungle'. On Chota Basdia, one of the Rabnabad islands, J.C. Panioty was given Rs. 3000 after submitting a petition explaining that his estate would be deserted 'unless new tenants are brought from other parts of the country and get money advanced to them to purchase agricultural implements and cattle'. Once the landlords had received the money, of course, they were free to lend it to the cultivators at whatever rate they pleased, or to spend it on something else entirely.

In Noakhali nearly 400 cultivators had visited Sudharam to petition for advances. Porch, however, had decided that there was 'no sign of such advances being really required'. A special inquiry into char Darvesh, a government estate on the coast, had in fact found that about 10 per cent of the tenants were in need of loans to buy plough cattle. The cost of these loans would have been about Rs. 1400. But the cultivators had fallen behind in their rent payments after the cyclone, and under the terms of the Land Improvement Act the government couldn't advance them the money. The legal absurdity was only a convenient pretext. The government didn't want to lend to the cultivators, and the result was that they became even more indebted to the moneylenders and landlords (roles often combined in the same person) than they had been before the cyclone.

Temple had been very clear in his instructions after the cyclone that no remissions of land revenue would be granted. Suggestions from relief officers that remissions might actually be necessary in the worst-affected estates were met with a reminder that the revenue demand had been fixed 'on the understanding that the zamindar is from the profits of good years to pay the revenues of bad ones'. And this principle was upheld by the Board of Revenue. The Board did, however, agree to suspend the revenue demand on those estates that had suffered most from the cyclone and storm-wave. In Chittagong the sum of the suspended revenues was Rs. 6000; in Noakhali, Rs. 16,000; and in Bakarganj the much greater sum of Rs. 171,000.

These revenue suspensions were granted on the condition that the zamindars shouldn't press the suffering cultivators for rent.

As with most of the zamindars' affairs, it is impossible to tell from the official records what actually happened. The government's approach on its own estates varied. Ebenezer Barton, the collector of Bakarganj, recommended a suspension of rents on Dakhin Shahbazpur. 'A two-anna crop following the general destruction of the storm-wave distinctly means the deep impoverishment of our ryots, if not something worse. I am by no means certain that as the year advances the ryots will be able to pay their rents.' Frederick Peacock, the divisional commissioner, agreed. The postponement of the rent demand, he said, was an 'act of clemency' that would also stop the cultivators from abandoning their holdings. Suspensions were also granted in the forest clearings of the mainland: the government didn't want to see the Sundarbans estates going back to jungle. In Noakhali, though, Porch thought that cultivators on the government's estates 'were able to pay their rents without difficulty' and should simply be told to 'make the necessary arrangements'.

It is possible that the cyclone did not, in the end, cause the government any great loss of revenue except on its own estates. It would certainly have affected the rent collections of the zamindars and superior tenure-holders. But it was the cultivators who suffered the most. Not only did they have to find the money to buy new ploughs and cattle, but they also had to pay their rents from the proceeds of their badly damaged crops. The landlords and moneylenders were waiting.

ભ

In January 1877 Sir Richard Temple had been appointed as the government of India's famine delegate to Madras. The appointment had been made on the understanding that he would apply to that presidency the same uncompromising free-market principles he had insisted on after the cyclone of 1876. By refusing all but the most superficial government aid to the victims of the cyclone, he had shown that he had learnt from the scandal of the 1873–74 Bengal famine. He had shown that he deserved another chance. And he had been given one: his response to the cyclone had been recognised by a promotion and the chance to manage a calamity of an even greater magnitude.

Lord Lytton—governor general, poetaster, and fanatical proponent of laissez-faire—had chosen his representative carefully. He could not, he told the India Office, have found 'a man more likely, or better able to help us save money in famine management'. (The reason why money needed to be saved, Lytton's finance minister, John Strachey, kept reminding him, was so the government could afford its planned invasion of Afghanistan.) Lytton's instructions to Temple on how to reduce famine spending hardly needed to be given, so closely did they follow the spirit of Temple's instructions to his subordinates after the cyclone. Still Lytton delivered the familiar sermon. 'It is essential in the present state of the finances that the most severe economy should be practised ... Even, however, if financial considerations were less overpoweringly strong, it would still be true that a Government has no better right in times of scarcity than in other times to attempt the task of preventing all suffering.' In practical terms this meant that Temple was to reduce the number of people on relief works; to stop the Madras government from purchasing grain reserves; and to ensure that private trade was allowed to take its course 'perfectly unfettered'.

Just as he had done after the cyclone, Temple made a brief tour of the affected areas. Again he had reached his conclusions before he set out. 'He expected to see a certain state of things,' the journalist William Digby wrote, 'and he saw that—that and none other.' One of his first decisions was to turn half a million people out of relief works. Access to the works was made as difficult as possible: people were forced to travel to distant relief camps instead of joining projects near their homes, and were not allowed to start work until they were nearly exhausted by hunger. As an 'experiment', the ration for male labourers was cut to a pound of rice a day. William Cornish, the Madras sanitary commissioner, thought that the one-pound ration—which became known as 'the Temple wage'—was an experiment certain to result in starvation. But Temple prevailed. One satirist, in response, drew up the 'Anti-Charitable Contributions Act, 1877', which banned private donations to famine relief and was signed in 'Inhumanville'.

The Bengali vernacular newspapers were appalled, but not entirely surprised, by Temple's relief reforms. 'We had the impression', *Amrita Bazar Patrika* wrote, 'that, in the opinion of the British nation, India was a promising field for all sorts of experiments; it is, however, now found that it is more; and that the lives of its inhabitants are supposed to be of even less value than toys.' *Bharat Sangskarak* reminded its readers of the feasting and celebrations that the rulers, now delivering sermons on austerity, had so recently been enjoying in Delhi. 'Such an exhibition of heartlessness was certainly not looked for so soon after the spectacle of an assemblage, on which public funds had been needlessly expended.' The *Hindu Hitoishini* compared Temple's actions to 'gilt ornaments, which take in people by their glitter, but which do not possess any intrinsic worth'. 'If, as seems likely enough, owing to the rules of relief made by Sir Richard Temple, the scenes of the Orissa famine be re-enacted in Southern India, he will doubtless leave the country more famous than even Sir Cecil Beadon.' (Beadon was lieutenant governor when famine broke out in Orissa in 1866. He refused to import grain for relief, claiming that the difficulty would be met by the laws of supply and demand: a third of the population of Orissa died.) *Sadharani* also found Orissa an instructive point of comparison. 'The chief merit of this policy is that, whereas in the Orissa famine there were deaths because no relief was granted, in the present case people are being put to death by a slow process of starvation.' And the *Bharat Mihir* noted Temple's spectral progress from one scene of calamity to another. 'We saw Sir Richard's action in connection with the storm-wave in Burrisal; and now, again, we find him dealing with the famine in the Bombay and Madras Presidencies. Our acquaintance with him shows that there is but little difference between cruelty and his ideas of economy.'

As it happened, there was little difference between Temple's ideas of economy and mass starvation. The official estimate of the number of deaths during the famine of 1876–78 was five million. Temple blamed the victims of the famine for their laziness. 'The infatuation of these poor people in respect to eating the bread of idleness; their dread of marching on command to any distance from home; their preference often for extreme privation rather than submission to even simple and reasonable orders, can be fully believed only by those who have seen or personally known these things.' Besides, he added, most of the victims had been beggars or other social parasites; their deaths, 'which they brought upon themselves', had merely 'terminated lives of idleness and too often of crime'.

In the middle of June 1877 reports began to appear in the Bengali press of an approaching famine in Chittagong. The reports caused alarm: everybody knew what was happening in southern and western India. The *Grambarta Prakashika*, a paper notable for its attention to the problems of the cultivators, asked why the government hadn't shown any signs of activity. Famine might have been expected: the survivors of the cyclone and epidemic hadn't been able to cultivate their salt-damaged lands, and there had been massive exports of rice to the famine areas in Madras and Bombay. If the same precautions had been taken in Chittagong as during the famine of 1874, the paper wrote, the scarcity might have been averted. Chittagong had good port facilities, and importing rice wouldn't have been difficult.

'The produce of Bengal is so large,' the *Prakashika* thought, 'that a considerable distribution of it and proper precautions might obviate all danger of famine. Still it occurs after very short intervals.' The government's neglect of the problem was symbolised by the physical remoteness of its most important officials: Lord Lytton was in the hills of Simla, Ashley Eden in Darjeeling. 'We feel sure that if, instead of any intelligence of famine, some order had been received from England directing an increase of taxes, both of them would have come down, leaving their enjoyments on the hills, even in this very hot season of the year, and would not have neglected any means necessary to suck the blood of the people ... Our rulers pay but little regard to the responsibility resting on them relative to the protection of life; and that merely in words, not deeds.' *Amrita Bazar Patrika* added that the government had just brought in large sums from newly introduced land registration fees and a road tax, so there was no reason why it should allow the people to suffer from hunger.

As predicted, the situation in Chittagong became progressively worse. But still there were no signs of help from the government. People who were usually well off had been reduced to beggary, and there were reports that some had committed suicide. In late August the *Sadharani* carried a terse account from its correspondent in the district. 'The condition of the people is daily becoming increasingly deplorable. Want is increasing. The amun seedlings have been transplanted, but agricultural operations are not progressing satisfactorily. The soil is still saturated with salt, and its productive powers have consequently diminished. It has been raining incessantly since last week, thus causing floods, owing to which the paddy seedlings are in danger of rotting in the fields. Ploughing cannot go on; and the roads are all laid under water. The people are crying for want of food in all directions. Should any respectable-looking man chance to pass through a village, the inhabitants—the old, and the women and children—all come out to beg alms. For want of sufficient food, the peasants have become weak, shrivelled, and emaciated, and are daily becoming incapable of active work.'

These were the circumstances in which the lieutenant governor, Ashley Eden, came down from the hills to give a speech on the 'disloyalty' of the vernacular newspapers. In it he cited the excellent condition of the Bengali peasantry, who he said were 'well fed, well clothed, and as happy as the peasantry of any other country in the world'. Unsurprisingly, the vernacular press responded energetically to this claim and to his criticisms of their attitude. 'Does Mr. Eden now really see the Bengal peasantry living in two-storied brick buildings instead of thatched huts?' the *Sambad Prabhakar* asked. 'Do they not really any longer borrow off the mahajuns [moneylenders] at 200 per cent. interest? ... Who will believe that the peasantry are happy when, on the first approach of famine, they have to dispose of their cattle and ploughs and repair to a relief station?'

As for Eden's remarks about the press, the paper explained that 'the native newspapers are impartial critics, while the Government of the country is a despotism: and so it is utterly impossible that there should be any agreement of views between the two'. The *Dacca Prakash* was equally forthright. 'The country is being daily impoverished through ... British enlightenment and British cunning. The people have become so poor, at the present time, that they live from hand to mouth; and the occurrence of the slightest natural calamity leaves them encumbered with debt ... Really, the saying that the peasantry are "well-fed and prosperous" amounts to nothing. We do not know what grounds Mr. Eden had for making such a remark, after his return from a visit as rare as that of a comet.'

The response to Eden's speech proved, to his mind, the truth of his charge, and it was not long before the Vernacular Press Act came into force. The Act was a response, he explained, to 'the sedition and gross disloyalty of some of the vernacular papers, and their attempts to sow the seeds of disaffection to British rule in the minds of ignorant people'. The government now had a way of repressing such writings and punishing their publishers.

The papers had said what they thought of the government's response to the cyclone and the famine, and what they thought of its expensive and unnecessary festivities. The barbs had found their mark. The vernacular papers were often misinformed, prejudiced one way or another, and wildly inconsistent in their views. But by giving their rulers an image of themselves in a different light they had done a job that the more moderate English-language Bengali press, and certainly the Anglo-Indian press, had studiously avoided.

™

One of the government's few constructive responses to the 1876 cyclone was the relocation of the subdivisional headquarters of Dakhin Shahbazpur. The old headquarters, Daulatkhan, on the island's eastern coast, had been destroyed by the storm-wave. A secondary aim of Peacock's November tour of the island—the primary one being to confirm that no more relief would be needed—was to find a safer location for a new headquarters town. The place that was selected was called Bhola. Bhola had a good trade in rice and betel nuts, and good connections with the rest of the island by water and road. It had a piece of higher land that would make a suitable site for the subdivisional buildings. And, most importantly, it was 4 miles inland.

The next step in restoring the island's administration was the appointment of a new subdivisional officer. The previous officer, Umacharan Banerjee, had gone on leave after losing his children and grandchildren on the night of the storm. It was his loss that gave Romesh Dutt, a man who was to become one of India's most influential critics of empire, what a biographer would later describe as 'his first great opportunity'.

When Dutt joined the Indian civil service in 1869 he became one of only five Indians to have done so since competitive recruitment was introduced in 1853. Two of them had been his companions when, as a nineteen-year old, he had run away from home to sail for England. (His conservative Hindu grandfather had refused to let him go overseas.) After a year's study he and his friends sat the civil service examination, and passed. By the time Dutt was sent to Dakhin Shahbazpur he had had several years' experience as a civil servant in various districts of Bengal, including as a famine relief officer in Nadia in 1874. But nothing he had studied or experienced could have prepared him for what he saw when he arrived on the island: it was a scene, he wrote in his memoir, 'which can never be forgotten'.

In April 1877, several months after he had arrived on Dakhin Shahbazpur, Dutt wrote to Barton describing the worsening situation and recommending that relief measures be introduced. The crops had failed. The cultivators of Barhanuddin, in the southern part of the island, had got little more than 2 annas, or an eighth, of what they had planted. Few people had rice in their homes: most were living, as they had been since the storm-wave, on rice bought from the markets. Since December it had been obvious that the harvest wouldn't be enough to feed everybody. The authorities had relied on private trade to supply the shortfall, thinking that the people, with their savings from past years and their stocks of betel nuts, would have enough money to buy rice brought in from outside the subdivision.

Dutt was familiar with the gospel of the free market, and indeed professed to follow it himself. 'I would on no account recommend interference with private trade, which, I believe, will always suffice to meet the demands of the people.' But unlike the authorities, his allegiance to the principles of free trade didn't stop him from realising that the market had its practical limits. Most people had by now sold everything they had: their betel nuts, their money and silver ornaments, the milk from their cows, even their firewood. 'It will thus be seen that a portion at least of the people are depending on precarious means of existence. The time has come for Government to provide them with works.'

Dutt proposed building two roads in Barhanuddin, and having canals dug as well. 'By spending money on these useful works, we keep off the necessity of relief operations in the present year.' He started on the works before getting Barton's permission: large crowds of people turned up. The road and canal projects, he thought, together with the advances and other relief already given, would get the people through the three months until the harvest of the autumn paddy. If the harvest was fair there would be no need for anxiety. But if the crops failed again, he warned, 'relief works on a very extensive scale will have to be undertaken'.

The works Dutt had begun could only support able-bodied men and their families. Halfway through the three months it became clear that people would soon start dying of starvation if the government didn't intervene. 'There are people who even now do not get their meals every day, who have no relatives to depend upon, and whom their neighbours are unable and unwilling to support.' Those in greatest distress were the poor and the home-less, disabled beggars, old men with no relatives, widows with children to support—people whose subsistence was uncertain even at the best of times. Dutt thought the distribution of rice to these people was 'imperatively needed' and should begin at once.

Dutt proposed to set up eight relief centres on the island, each feeding about 250 people a day until the autumn harvest. The total cost of the scheme would be Rs. 7900: these calculations supposed that the distressed people would have their midday meal in the relief centres and take away cooked rice for their evening meal at home. But Rs. 7900 was much more than was left in the subscribed relief fund. Dutt had about Rs. 2000, and thought that Barton could send him another Rs. 1000 if needed.

This left a shortfall of nearly Rs. 5000. 'I have no doubt that in the present very critical and distressed circumstances of this sub-division, Government will grant this small sum to save life and relieve those who are in utter distress.'

Getting the government to grant any sum turned out to be harder than Dutt expected. Barton, in a letter to Peacock, wrote that he could not recommend the distribution of rice. 'We should have to support all the beggars in the sub-division, who of course would cease to beg or exert themselves in any way to keep themselves alive.' He did agree to send Dutt the balance of the subscribed relief fund, about Rs. 1500, from the treasury. But the Rs. 4900 that Dutt had asked for could not be given. The government, he said, had 'done so much this year for the distressed people of Dakhin Shahbazpore' that they couldn't 'reasonably' expect any more: it was a remark that could have come from the pages of *Oliver Twist*. Dutt could, however, use the money he had to implement a skeleton version of his scheme. 'Perhaps,' Barton wrote, 'in order to prevent a few deaths, it might be as well to open three or four centres where cooked food could be distributed.'

After receiving Barton's sceptical response to his proposal, Dutt carried out further inquiries into the condition of the people of Dakhin Shahbazpur. These confirmed his earlier view that there was great distress among the poorer classes, and that it was likely to increase over the next two months. 'Widows who by the late cyclone or cholera have been left helpless with a number of children to support, wives whose husbands are infirm or diseased and incapable of work, orphans who since the cyclone have depended on the charity of others, old men with no near relatives to support them, and people generally who are incapable of work and have habitually depended on others, all these are now greatly distressed and pinched for food.' Many were going a day or two without rice and subsisting in between on gourds. 'I have walked into houses just at the time of cooking, noon, without previous intimation of my coming. I have sometimes found entire families having not a morsel of rice in their house, and boiling some kumra [a type of gourd] only to live upon for that day.'

The distribution of cooked rice to these people, Dutt wrote, was 'an absolute and urgent necessity'. But he knew that he had to overcome Barton's concerns about the rice being given to 'beggars'. 'I apprehend serious loss of life during the next two months unless the measure is commenced at once. You apprehend that the measure will merely bring on our hands all the beggars of the sub-division.' That might happen, but at a time when begging was becoming more and more uncertain as a means of subsistence, 'any scheme for saving lives must include those who are beggars, not by choice, but by necessity'. And beggars of any kind would make up a small percentage of those relieved. Most would be the families of cultivators and labourers who had been reduced to distress by the storm-wave and epidemic.

Barton was still reluctant to admit the existence of a serious problem. The enthusiasm for relief schemes he had shown immediately after the storm had evaporated. Perhaps he felt he was being upstaged by his Bengali subordinate: the benign paternalism of the district officer, after all, was dependent on his absolute power. He now claimed to find it 'satisfactory' that 'the very poorest classes in the sub-division can live on lau [another type of gourd] and kumra'. And, extraordinarily, he added that it might not be a bad thing if a few people did starve to death. 'The abundance of vegetables and fruit should, in my opinion, prevent deaths from starvation, but perhaps at present it might be well to risk the occurrence of these.'

Dutt did everything he could in difficult circumstances. He opened four relief centres for distributing cooked rice, cutting the ration to one meal a day for adults to fit within the restricted budget. (Children were given enough rice to take home for a second meal at night.) On the first few days the centres were open they fed nearly 400 people a day. Many more came for relief but had to be turned away so that rice could be given to the 'utterly destitute and helpless'. As the establishment of the centres became more widely known, the numbers applying for relief increased. Dutt's analysis of the situation had been confirmed by events, and he was allowed to open another two centres. By mid-July the centres were supplying food to nearly 1500 people a day.

Dutt kept records of the religion, sex, and age of the people applying for relief. Among the Hindus relieved on 14 July were 63 men, 125 women, and 127 children. Among the Muslims were 235 men, 111 women, and 793 children. The proportions stayed the same throughout the week. Hindus made up only 17 per cent of the island's population; the high number applying for relief suggests that the mainly Hindu artisan classes, who had no stocks of rice—barbers, carpenters, blacksmiths, potters, fishermen, washermen—suffered more than the mainly Muslim cultivators. The much greater number of men than women in the Muslim figures, and its reverse in the Hindu figures, may point to the limitations on women's movements under purdah. The large number of Muslim children being provided with relief is harder to explain. Apart from the fact that Muslim families usually had more children than Hindus, it may suggest that some of the food the children took home was going to their house-bound mothers.

Dutt's final report in the official proceedings was sent to Barton just before the harvest of the autumn paddy. Distress had become universal, but deaths from starvation had been averted. There was still a shortage of food in the outlying areas, especially on the chars. Modhusudan Sarkar, a local official, found a group of families on one char who hadn't had any rice for three days: the children were 'crying with hunger', and the adults 'looked half starved and prostrate'. In other families the children were living on a kind of aquatic weed. With the harvest, though, the worst of the distress seems to have passed.

The eventual success of the relief measures on Dakhin Shahbazpur was a result of Dutt's initiative and tenacity, his courage in speaking up to his district officer, and his ability to make a convincing case within the limits of official protocol. When he returned to Dakhin Shahbazpur as the collector of Bakarganj in 1883 he found that he was remembered with gratitude. His welcome, he wrote to his brother, seemed to him 'far more sincere than many ovations which are got up and organised in more civilised places for higher officials'—such as, perhaps, the durbar of 1 January 1877, when he had had to leave the desolated island for the celebrations in Barisal. This time, before he left again for Barisal, the residents of Bhola put on a historical play for him. It was a good choice: history was his favourite literary form.

Dutt is still remembered for his two-volume economic history of India under British rule. In these books he argued that the impoverishment of India was the responsibility of its rulers. 'It would be a sad story for future historians to tell', he wrote in the second volume, 'that the Empire gave the people of India peace but not prosperity; that the manufacturers lost their industries; that the cultivators were ground down by a heavy and variable taxation which precluded any saving; that the revenues of the country were to a large extent diverted to England; and that recurring and desolating famines swept away millions of the population.' A sad story—but one that has proven hard to disclaim.

ᘓᗺ

The government was still worried about the state of law and order in the cyclone-affected districts. In April 1877 Porch received strict orders about the suppression of dacoity in Noakhali, along with a reminder that he would be held responsible if crime went unchecked. The police, he thought, hadn't been nearly active enough in watching the movements of 'bad characters' after the cyclone. From now on, he told the superintendent, the police should follow more closely the activities of known criminals, recording any suspicious movements, keeping an ear out for any schemes, and noting any meetings that took place among them, whether in houses or at the markets.

There were several reasons, Porch thought, why crime might have increased in the aftermath of the disaster. Many criminals had escaped or been released from jail on the night of the storm; the lawlessness immediately afterwards had revived the 'thieving spirit' of the people; the lower classes had been left badly off; and the village watch had virtually collapsed.

The annual reports on the administration of criminal justice in Bengal show that the number of offences recorded in Noakhali decreased in 1877–78 and again in 1878–79. Porch thought that would-be criminals had been put off by the harsher punishments—more floggings—being imposed. More convictions had also been achieved, which he attributed to better discipline among the police. Whatever was behind the favourable figures, they gave him a rare and much-needed example of administrative success.

A slight increase in the number of offences was recorded in Chittagong after the cyclone. An especially grotesque injustice was the prosecution under the Salt Act of cultivators who had lost their crops to the storm-wave and were trying to turn the pools of salt water on their land to use. The desperate state of the people after the failure of their crops was also identified as a reason for the increase in the number of crimes. One emaciated offender, sentenced to flogging for stealing paddy from the fields, asked to be put into prison instead so that he might have something to eat.

The situation in Bakarganj was quite different from Noakhali and Chittagong. According to the report on criminal administration for 1877–78, no district in Bengal had recorded a greater number of riots, murders, or dacoities. 'The district is literally all ablaze with lawlessness', the judge of Bakarganj wrote. Peacock was asked to explain. He couldn't account for the cases of murder and riot, but thought that the dacoities might have been related to the high food prices since the cyclone. Eden didn't believe him. The cyclone had been a serious calamity, he wrote, but it had been limited in extent, and had happened more than eighteen months ago. Peacock answered that although the cyclone was perhaps not the immediate cause of the problem, the people in the affected area, which covered most of the south of the district, hadn't yet recovered from their losses. Their difficulties had been compounded by poor rains in 1877, which together with large exports of paddy from the district had kept prices high.

Eden sent the deputy inspector-general of police to Bakarganj to investigate. The increase in cases of dacoity, the officer reported, was simply because of a change in the way such incidents were categorised, not an actual increase in criminal activity. The increase in riot cases, though, could be attributed to the misconduct and inefficiency of the investigating officers. 'Some are lazy and dilatory, some ignorant and stupid, and many excessively corrupt.' Long delays in bringing rioters to court had led the landlords and their retainers to think that they could get away with anything. Officers had built up connections with criminals. The local knowledge that the village watchmen were supposed to supply wasn't being properly used. And the district's status as a hardship posting meant that it had become a destination for the inexperienced and those who had failed or misbehaved elsewhere.

A final report on the subject was prepared by James Monro, the inspector-general of police. Monro accepted Peacock's explanation. Many parts of the district, he wrote, had still not recovered from the effects of the cyclone. The harvest in 1877 had been poor, the prospects for this year were discouraging, and rice was selling at famine rates. The zamindars and superior tenure-holders were finding it hard to bring in their rents. This explained the increase in the number of riots: the zamindars were able to employ clubmen with even greater ease than usual, and had been using them to collect their dues. There were also numerous property disputes, especially over cattle which had been swept to distant parts and were now being reclaimed by their former owners.

Despite Monro's analysis of the situation, his proposed solution had nothing to do with the problems the district was facing after the cyclone. Instead he recommended that the police force should be strengthened: seven additional sub-inspectors and fifty constables should be appointed for at least a year, and a fleet of new patrol boats should be introduced to prevent dacoity on the rivers and creeks. He had strong words for H.N. Harris, the former superintendent of police who had recently been promoted. Through 'carelessness and maladministration', Monro said, Harris had let the district fall into lawlessness. 'I think that he should be brought to account', he told Eden.

Eden said that if he had had any idea of the disgraceful state of the police in Bakarganj he would never have approved Harris's promotion. But some of the blame, he thought, must also be placed on Barton, the magistrate. He found this conclusion hard to reconcile with reports of Barton's ability and energy. But the administration of Bakarganj had become 'a public scandal', and if Barton couldn't explain he would be demoted to a lower grade of the service.

Once again Barton found himself in trouble with the province's highest authority. First it had been Sir Richard Temple, reprimanding him for giving money to the destitute and starving after the cyclone. Now it was Sir Ashley Eden, blaming him for an increase in crimes that were quite likely being committed by the very people Temple had refused to help. In his defence, Barton explained that he had been burdened with work under the Land Registration Act, which had come into force in 1876: the endless subdivision of property in Bakarganj made accurate registration almost impossible. There had also been the implementation of the road tax, which had given a great deal of trouble. His official duties had been so heavy that he hadn't been able to properly supervise Harris and the police.

The results of this 'public scandal' were an increase in the number of police and stricter measures against criminals. Opinions that linked the increase in crime to the effects of the cyclone were put to one side: to acknowledge them would have been to acknowledge that the district hadn't yet made the recovery claimed for it.

CR

The scale of the destruction caused by the cyclone and storm-wave made it impossible to avoid the question of whether such a disaster could be prevented from happening again. Temple, at least, didn't think so. 'I know not how to devise such a safeguard, nor have I seen anyone who can suggest anything', he wrote in his minute of November 1876. The area exposed to the waves was too large to be protected by embankments, and even if such protective works were built they would, if breached, do more harm than good by stopping the salt water from running off the fields. Besides, he added, disasters like that of 1876 didn't happen very often.

Shortly after the publication of Temple's minute the question of protection from storm-waves was taken up in *The Times*. In a letter to the paper William Cornish, the sanitary commissioner of Madras, suggested that a new technique of house construction should be adopted in the cyclone-prone districts. The existing houses were poorly suited to conditions on the coast: they were single-storied, made of mat and thatch, built on elevated mounds where naturally available, otherwise raised on mud platforms only a couple of feet high. An alternative model could be found in the houses of the Burmese, built on wooden piles that raised the floor of the house 10 to 15 feet above the ground. What Cornish didn't know was that this technique was already in use among the Burmese Maghs living on the Bakarganj coast. Together with the protective belts of forest around their settlements, it had served them well during the storm-wave. Krishna Gupta, the subdivisional officer of Patuakhali, had even suggested in one of his letters to Barton that the Bengalis should adopt a few of the Magh habits, which seemed 'well adapted to the nature of the country'.

Another scheme for saving lives was put forward by H.J. Rainey, a grant-holder from Jessore. Rainey thought that the best solution would be to build pucka masonry buildings with high rooftops that people could climb onto. But the expense of this would be more than the government or the people—or a combination of both—could afford. What was needed was a cheaper structure that could be built without skilled labour. Rainey suggested that the inhabitants of the coast should be required, with whatever financial help the government and land-owners could give them, to build within a mile or so of each village a large earthen mound. The mound should be higher than the reach of any storm-wave, and big enough to accommodate all the inhabitants of the village on top. Its sides should be sloped for stability, and to let women and children (and perhaps cattle too) get up without difficulty. A low, solid shed on top would provide shelter to women, children, and the infirm; further protection from the wind and water could be gained by planting a barrier of silk-cotton and tamarind trees around its base.

After reading Temple's minute the Sundarbans commissioner, A.D.B. Gomess, wrote to the government reminding it of the protective works on Sagar Island. Between 1811 and 1867 this island in the mouth of the Hooghly river had been struck by six major cyclones. Two of them, in 1833 and 1864, had taken thousands of lives. After 1864 the government had offered to give up part of the island's revenues if the proprietors agreed to build and maintain protective works for their tenants. Each village would have a small tank surrounded by embankments high and strong enough to survive a storm-wave. The inner slope of the embankment and a margin of flat land around the tank would provide a place of refuge. No house would be more than a mile from the enclosure, and roads leading from the village to the enclosure would be built at the proprietor's expense. Similar works, Gomess thought, might save many lives on the eastern seaboard. (He didn't mention that on three of Sagar Island's four estates the enclosures existed only on paper.)

Fleetwood Pellew had been the government's special relief officer on Sandwip and Hatia. In the centre of these islands, he wrote, there were several large tanks with embankments around them. Most were in poor repair, and he didn't see one that hadn't been breached by the flood. But on the night of the storm many people had found refuge on them, and if the embankments had been stronger, or the flood less violent, they might have found good water too. Pellew suggested that these tanks should be repaired and others built near the coast where they were now scarce. He had seen Rainey's suggestion of solid mounds, and thought that tanks were far superior: they contained a supply of fresh water for the people who were rescued, and there was no difficulty in getting enough earth for the embankments: it would come from the tank itself.

The existence of well-embanked, if crumbling, tanks in the centre of Sandwip suggests that the people of the estuary might once have been better protected from storm-waves than they were in 1876. There was further evidence of an early system of protective works on the Noakhali mainland, where a cordon of embanked tanks ran along an old road many miles inland. The tanks were of a great size, and must have been built to withstand floods and storm-waves along what was once the coast. They were well beyond the ability of villagers to build and maintain, and had probably been financed by a state less reluctant to invest in public works than the British. As the mainland had pushed out into the sea, with new chars being formed and new settlements established on them, no new cordon had been built. The line of old tanks was a reminder that in more than a hundred years of collecting Noakhali's taxes, the British had not taken even the most elementary measures to keep their subjects from being destroyed by the storm-waves of the Bay of Bengal.

CR

For a short time after the 1876 cyclone it seemed as though that habit of neglect was about to change. After considering the various suggestions that had been made, Eden ordered an inquiry into whether embanked enclosures of the kind already on Sagar Island and Sandwip could be built along the eastern seaboard.

In Bakarganj Barton travelled through a good part of the wave-affected area with his deputy Kedarnath Ghose, consulting landlords and their agents and talking to the village headmen. It became clear—if it hadn't been already—that the main problem would be financing the works. The landlords were reluctant to pay. 'All of them plead a thousand excuses and try to shirk off the burden from their shoulders. Of course they would be only too thankful if the work is done for them.' Barton knew that the landlords, especially the owners of small estates and under-tenures—by far the most numerous class of landowners in Bakarganj—had suffered financially from the cyclone and cholera epidemic, and that it would be a long time before they recovered. But, he added, they owed a duty to their tenants that they shouldn't avoid.

Barton was equally unimpressed with the attitude of the tenants, who seemed to him 'extremely apathetic'. 'If anything is done for them, well and good, but to combine and exert together even in a thing which is quite necessary to save their lives, is out of the question. They would rather wait quietly to be swept away by another wave than make any determined efforts to avoid such a catastrophe.' Neither the tenants nor their landlords, he concluded, would supply the labour and capital needed for the works unless they were compelled to by law.

The district's unusual pattern of settlement also gave Barton reason to doubt the practicality of the tanks. Bakarganj had no villages in the ordinary sense—each homestead stood on its own, surrounded by its garden and moat and separated from the next one by paddy fields. Where, in such thinly populated settlements, could the tanks be built so as to be within reach of all the inhabitants?

Porch's contribution to the inquiry was carried out in his usual peremptory manner. He had firm views on the subject: only a few months before the cyclone he had described the idea of building embankments along the Meghna as 'absurd'. The drowning of some 90,000 people in his district hadn't changed his mind. The question of fully embanking the district wasn't within the terms of the inquiry, but he felt the need to object to it again, this time on the grounds that embankments stopped water from flowing off the land. Enclosed tanks were dismissed as 'too costly in character, and of very doubtful expediency'. His pronouncements on the number of tanks required, their cost, and their practicality were unsupported by any evidence or expert opinion: when the divisional commissioner asked whether he had consulted the executive engineer at Chittagong, as he had been told to, Porch admitted that he hadn't. There had been no need to, he explained, because he had already decided that the proposals shouldn't be carried out.

After a long delay, in 1880 the government issued a resolution that embanked tanks should be constructed along all parts of the coast exposed to storm-waves. In practice this meant the three eastern districts of Bakarganj, Noakhali, and Chittagong: Midnapur, in the west, had a sea-wall, and the southern faces of the 24 Parganas and Jessore were protected by the Sundarbans. The tanks were to be built by the landowners; the government should set an example to the rest by building them first on its own estates. Yet the resolution, a member of the Board of Revenue later remarked, was 'merely ... a counsel of perfection'. The only example the government set was one of inaction; and the other landlords were only too happy to follow.

A correspondent to *The Times* had written in January 1877 that the construction of protective works 'would nullify the fatal forgetfulness of the past which endangers a people without records'. The debate over such works in the aftermath of the 1876 cyclone showed that people could be endangered just as effectively by a government that had no shortage of records, but for the sake of its own finances was only too willing to ignore them.

☙

Another subject of discussion in the aftermath of the storm was whether people could be given early warning of approaching cyclones. Traditional warning signs included dogs howling, the leaves of the silk-cotton tree turning upside down, and ants moving to higher ground. On Sandwip and Hatia people had heard a roaring sound coming from the Bay of Bengal for two or three days before the cyclone, and a few had saved themselves and their families by building plantain rafts and tying them with long ropes to trees in their homesteads.

One correspondent to *The Times* thought that a scientific system of warnings could be introduced if India's meteorological observatories were better organised. In Europe and North

America the recently introduced system of weather charts and storm warnings had been a success: nearly 80 per cent of warnings issued by Britain's Meteorological Office in 1873 and 1874 had been justified by events. If India's existing meteorological stations were properly organised and equipped, the correspondent wrote, such results, in India's more regular climate, might be equalled if not bettered.

A response to this letter came from Richard Strachey, a prominent scientist and administrator in India. Strachey explained that the government was already taking an interest in Indian meteorology. A meteorological service had recently been established, and would eventually produce useful results. India's telegraphy, though, wasn't as highly developed as Britain's, and tropical cyclones presented meteorological problems that didn't apply to European storms. It was unlikely, Strachey thought, that any warning system would be able to prevent the repetition of a disaster like that of 1876.

Another perspective on the problem was offered by the government of Bengal's meteorological reporter, John Elliott. Elliott wrote that he found it hard to make much progress in studying storms with such a small department, and that his teaching duties in Calcutta reduced the time he could spend on the work. Knowledge of the Bay of Bengal's meteorology remained 'extremely limited'. The reliable forecasting of cyclones in the bay, he concluded, was waiting on both theoretical and practical developments: a better understanding of their origin and causes, and the extension of the telegraph to Port Blair in the Andaman Islands, the area where cyclones usually formed.

Neither Elliott nor Strachey mentioned that Calcutta was already protected by a system of storm-warnings. The system had been introduced after the cyclone of 1864, which had caused great damage to shipping in the port. Observers were sent to several stations along the coast of the bay: Sagar Island, False

159

Point, Chittagong, Akyab, and Cuttack. They were given instruments for measuring the air pressure, humidity, and rainfall, and told to report their readings twice a day by telegraph, along with an estimate of the direction and force of the wind and any general observations about the weather. Their reports were passed on to the master attendant of the port, who raised the appropriate signals, and also to the newspapers. Special attention was given to the system during the cyclone seasons. And it worked well, allowing a warning of several hours to be given to shipping in the port of the cyclone of November 1867.

There was no warning system for the Meghna estuary. Calcutta was further inland and easier to warn than the settlements along the coast. It was also the capital of British India. The districts of eastern Bengal were a long way down the imperial hierarchy of places. They suffered more than anywhere else from the effects of cyclones, but would be the last to benefit from any advances in cyclone meteorology.

If warnings couldn't be given and protective works couldn't be built, the correspondent to *The Times* had written, 'the Government, who must have long since realized the possibility of the submersion of these low-lying spots, and who have left the inhabitants at the mercy of the waves ... should answer for their inaction'. Two years ago, when news of the Bengal famine reached England, another correspondent had called for the impeachment of the governor general if a single person died of hunger. 'What does this correspondent think of 120,000 lives sacrificed to official apathy? In no other civilized country in the world could such havoc occur without eliciting the most strenuous efforts of those in power to prevent recurrence of it; but in India the direst catastrophes, though repeated year by year, raise but a transitory interest.'

CR

The census of 1881 showed a slight increase in the population of Bakarganj since the last count in 1872. It was, the author of the census report thought, 'a remarkable proof of the recuperative powers of the people of Bengal and their rapid increase after calamity'. Credit was also due to the government, which had made 'great efforts' to 'succour the distressed': five years after the cyclone, official fantasies were becoming official history. Most of the increase had in fact been made in parts of the district that had escaped the storm-wave: the population of Bhola had decreased by 11 per cent, Bauphal by 20 per cent, and Golachipa by 25 per cent. The situation was similar in Noakhali, where the population as a whole had slightly decreased and the southern divisions had fallen by 15 to 25 per cent.

The next census, ten years later, showed a more convincing demographic recovery. There had been an increase of 18 per cent across Bakarganj, and the divisions on the coast had grown by as much as 40 per cent. Some of this increase was from internal migration, as people from the northern divisions moved to the now empty lands in the south and east. Most of the migrants were Muslims. 'Whether it be that the migratory instinct be stronger among them', the collector wrote, 'or they are more possessed with the spirit of enterprise and independence, the fact is that the Musalmans are much more ready to move on, while the Hindus cling to their homes in the north.' Most of the emigrants from Dacca and Faridpur were also Muslims. On Bhola (formerly Dakhin Shahbazpur), the Muslim population had grown from 91,000 in 1872 to 126,000 in 1891, while the Hindu population had actually decreased, from 24,000 to 18,000. The same pattern could be seen in Golachipa and Barhanuddin. The cyclone had intensified a trend in the religious demography of Bakarganj in which the south of the district, with its chars and forest clearings, became ever more Islamic.

Noakhali in 1891 showed the greatest population increase of any district in Bengal. The superintendent of the census,

C.J. O'Donnell (who since publishing his anonymous attack on Sir Richard Temple had prospered in the civil service) thought that the increase had more to do with the 'great fecundity' of the Muslim cultivators than with migration. Yet fifteen years after the cyclone, the population of Hatia was still less than it had been in 1872: the surviving men, one official noted, had had great difficulty in attracting wives to the island.

Traces of the disaster's long-term effects can also be found in the records of the Bakarganj cadastral survey, carried out some thirty years after the cyclone. The heavy volumes of survey sheets—many of which are held together by little more than grime and cobwebs—are kept in the deputy commissioner's record room at Barisal. Of the areas worst affected by the cyclone, only the volumes for Bauphal and Barhanuddin still exist. They show that the cyclone remained a defining moment in the collective consciousness: events of special importance, whether dacoities, murders, or the purchase of tenures, were reported to the settlement officer as having happened before or after 'the great flood'. They also show that the storm-wave had changed the topography of the estuary, causing the Tetulia river to silt up faster and the Deula river to dry up completely. Entire villages had since been established in their abandoned beds. One survey officer even thought that these changes had helped to lower the crime rate. 'Of late years no special or large riot has taken place, but years ago this village was in a most lawless state ... since the great flood communication has been opened out and thus crime has reduced.'

The pattern of life on the estuary's chars and islands hadn't changed much since 1876. Cultivators on the older formations, further inland and with more fertile soil, were usually described as being reasonably well off. Yet even there the oppressive consequences of subdivided land tenure were still being felt. On Manpura, for instance, the survey officer found that the tenure system was encouraging rack-renting—the same observation

William Dampier had made seventy-five years earlier. On another well-established estate the lease-holders were described as doing their best 'to realise as much as they can and spend as little as possible'. 'They are traders and deal in money-lending business. The interests of the actual cultivators of the soil are not safe in their hands. The lease-holders have grown fat and prosperous.'

The situation on the newly-formed chars was much worse. Char Padmamanasa, in the south of Dakhin Shahbazpur, had been colonised as recently as the 1880s. The soil was only 'middling', the settlement officer reported, and the tenants 'do not seem to be prosperous ... most of them are indebted to the local moneylenders, the tenure-holders'. In many parts salt-water flooding was a recurring problem. The tenants built small embankments along the creeks, but couldn't afford bigger ones that would keep the salt water off their crops. There was nothing to protect them from another storm-wave.

Char Bhuta, an estate on the coast of the Bay of Bengal, had lost over half its population to the storm-wave and much of the rest to the cholera epidemic. Since then it had been repopulated, though its inhabitants remained as exposed to disaster as ever. The landlord lived in Faridpur and was said to derive 'considerable profit' from the estate. The cultivators saw most of their income disappear into the middlemen's pockets. Additional taxes were levied 'whenever any suitable opportunity presents itself'. There was a scarcity of good drinking water: the landlord refused to dig a tank, and the tenants couldn't afford to. Cholera broke out every few years. There were no embankments and no forest—'the entire mouza [village] is a most open tract spreading out to sea'. The landlord made 'a good deal of money' by leasing new accretions to people whose houses and land elsewhere had been washed away by the rivers.

The storm-wave of 1876 had drowned many of the cultivators living on the grants and resumed estates of the Bakarganj

Sundarbans. Large areas of newly-cleared land had been thrown out of cultivation, and several grants had been sold for arrears of revenue. Even so, the government showed no sign of reconsidering its policy of total deforestation in the district. There was never any suggestion of replanting a belt of forest along the coast. Grants were still being given out on generous terms, both to big developers and to individual cultivators—although in practice the smaller grants usually ended up in the hands of the middlemen. The smaller grants had been introduced in the hope that they would result in the forest being cleared more quickly, and in this at least they were successful: in the years after the storm, the settlement officer James Jack wrote, 'a large area was brought under cultivation in a short time and the revenue obtained was very considerable'.

Perhaps the most notable consequence of the 1876 cyclone was the absence of any measures aimed at preventing a similar event in the future. There were no embankments, no storm warnings, no attempts at reforestation. Financial assistance was kept to an absolute minimum, and never reached those who had suffered most. The attitude of the government and the zamindars to the recovery was determined by the same calculus of risk and profit that had set the stage for disaster. Their interests went no further than the restoration of business as usual—the business of maximising revenue and rent. For those who cultivated the chars and the forest clearings, for all those who found themselves on this isolated and exposed coast, life remained a disaster waiting to happen.

EPILOGUE

THE TRIAL

The young woman, a prostitute, is crying: there is nothing left, the storm has swept everything away. She lifts her voice to Narayana, the preserver, 'the one who rests on water', who in the great flood that covered heaven, earth, and hell, took the form of a child and floated to safety on a banyan leaf.

'Lord Narayana,' the woman pleads, 'give us justice. We are living in fear. Even at night, when men and women are enjoying their most intimate moments, they are not without fear. Every child needs its mother's lap, but so many now are living without their mother's warmth ... Lord Narayana, give us justice.'

Hearing this, Narayana asks the woman to tell him more about the calamity.

'I was a resident of Dakhin Shahbazpur, and lived with a man who worked in Daulatkhan. On the day of the storm one could hardly make out whether it was day or night—the clouds covered the entire sky. Then it started to rain; it rained so hard that it seemed as though the entire earth might be destroyed. That night the moon and the stars were hidden; it was as dark as the darkest hour of a new moon night.

'The storm uprooted trees and ravaged the houses. It took things up in the air and threw them like a potter throwing his clay. The

whole earth shook. Then the waters of the rivers and sea came up. It was hard to tell the land from the sea. People were screaming. Some took shelter on the roofs of their houses; others climbed trees. Countless people drowned, gulping down salt water. Countless animals were washed away with them; the living world became a world of inanimate objects.

'An old man was crying: he could not find his sons. A mother was crying: she was lamenting her dead children. Children were crying: they could not find their parents. Wives were lamenting their husbands, and husbands were looking for their wives. The addicts and alcoholics were crying; even we, the prostitutes, were crying for our customers.

'Lord Narayana, the almighty has not been kind in taking away the lives of so many ordinary men and women. The storm plundered us like you plundered the demons of Lanka. The survivors now are dying of hunger. They are praying for some kind of sign or direction. Lord Narayana, give us justice.'

Narayana asks the woman to be patient for a little while. He will summon Paban, the god of wind and storm, and put him on trial for the destruction he has caused. A devotee is sent to fetch Paban. On seeing the messenger, Paban pretends to be ill, but is dragged before Narayana regardless. Narayana questions him. 'Is what I have heard true? Why did you do this?' Paban is evasive: 'What are you accusing me of? Do you have any witnesses?'

Narayana turns to the woman and asks her to suggest a suitable witness. The woman, though, decides that she will let Paban choose his own; that way there cannot be any doubt about the fairness of the verdict. Paban nominates Agni, the god of fire. The devotee, watching proceedings from the side, gives a little smile: Paban might think that Agni, being his friend, will take his side—but the devotee knows that Agni never lies.

Agni is lit, and bursts into flames. Narayana then asks: 'What exactly was Paban doing on 16 Kartik?' And Agni answers: 'That night, Paban was so violent that the fire could not be lit at all.'

NOTES

Abbreviations

ALA   Angus Library and Archive, Oxford
CSCR   Controller of Salt Chaukis Records, Letters Received from the
          Superintendent of the Salt Chaukis of Bullooah (Noakhali)
DCRR   Deputy Commissioner's Record Room
GoB   Government of Bengal
HDP/J   Home Department Proceedings, Judicial
IOR   India Office Records, British Library, London
L/PJ   Public and Judicial Department Records
NAI   National Archives of India, New Delhi
NDR   Noakhali District Records, National Archives of Bangladesh,
          Dhaka
PCSR   Presidency Commissioner Sundarbans Records, Old Disposed
          of Cases
RNN   Reports on Native Newspapers, Bengal
SDP/IS   Statistical Department Proceedings, Industry and Science
WBSA   West Bengal State Archives, Calcutta

Letters without any further reference are from the Financial Department
Proceedings, Industry and Science, held at the West Bengal State Archives,
Calcutta; letters with the reference FDP/M are from the Miscellaneous branch
of the same Department. The month of the volume is noted in square brackets when it differs from the month in which the letter was sent.

PREFACE

xi.   Cyclone of 1584: The version of this story in Beveridge's *District of Bakarganj* (1876), 27–8, is from Francis Gladwin's 1784 translation of the *Ain i Akbari*. The same passage is translated with slight differences by Henry Blochmann in the *Proceedings of the Asiatic Society of Bengal* (1868), 266–7, and by Jarrett in *The Ain i Akbari*, ii (1891), 123.

xi–xii. Rajas of Chandradwip: Beveridge, *The District of Bakarganj* (1876), 73; Bernier is quoted in Hunter, *A Statistical Account of Bengal*, vi (1876), 242.

xii. Kachua in 1874: Beveridge, *The District of Bakarganj* (1876), 73.

xiv. Calamity forgotten: Dambeck, 'The Great Bengal Cyclone of 1876' (1877), 192.

xiv. No lack of records: The only noteworthy work on cyclones in India is by the economic historian Tirthankar Roy, whose *Natural Disasters and Indian History* (2012) has a brief discussion of the 1876 storm based on the parliamentary papers published after the disaster.

xv.   Island disappearing: Smart is quoted in Gastrell, *Geographical and Statistical Report* (1868), 31.

1. THE ESTUARY

1–2. Hooker's journey: Hooker, *Himalayan Journals*, ii (1854), 337–44.

2.   Difficulties: Hunter, *A Statistical Account of Bengal*, vi (1876), 250.

2.   Tides: Beveridge, *The District of Bakarganj* (1876), 4–9.

2–3. Labour: Buchanan, *Francis Buchanan in Southeast Bengal* (1992), 139.

3.   Earnings and health: Hunter, *A Statistical Account of Bengal*, vi (1876), 256; Beveridge, *The District of Bakarganj* (1876), 12; Pogson, *Captain Pogson's Narrative* (1831), 23.

3.   Stimulants and accidents: Beveridge, *The District of Bakarganj* (1876), 15, 233–4, 255; Hunter, *A Statistical Account of Bengal*, vi (1876), 253.

3–4.   Great rivers: Jack, *Final Report* (1915), 5–6; Rennell, *Memoir of a Map of Hindoostan* (1793), 358.

4–5.   Creation and destruction: Rennell, *Memoir of a Map of Hindoostan* (1793), 341–7; 'Extract from Mr. R. Knox's Field Book', 1803, NAI, 35.

5.   Cyclones: Gastrell, *Geographical and Statistical Report* (1868), 28; Hooker, *Himalayan Journals*, ii (1854), 342.

5–6.   Land gaining on sea: Rennell, *Memoir of a Map of Hindoostan* (1793), 346–7.

6.   Land-building in Bakarganj: 'Extract from Mr. R. Knox's Field Book', NAI, 1803, 53; Gastrell, *Geographical and Statistical Report* (1868), 29–30; Pellew, 'Physical Characteristics of Backergunge' (1864), 200–1.

6–7.   Land-building in Noakhali: Sen, *Final Report* (1939), 9; Thompson, *Final Report* (1919), 8–15; Hunter, *A Statistical Account of Bengal*, vi (1876), 284.

7.   Absence of industry: Hunter, *A Statistical Account of Bengal*, vi (1876), 279, 321; Beveridge, *The District of Bakarganj* (1876), 298; Beverley, *Report on the Census of Bengal* (1872), 6–17, Statistical Returns, clxiv.

7.   Economic benefits of industry: Taylor, *A Sketch of the Topography and Statistics of Dacca* (1840), 161–4.

7–8.   East India Company: Bhattacharya and Chaudhuri, 'Regional Economy' (1983), 283–9; Mitra, *The Cotton Weavers of Bengal* (1978), 49–69.

8.   Zamindars and weavers: Hossain, 'The Alienation of Weavers' (1979), 336–40.

8.   Francis Buchanan: Buchanan, *Francis Buchanan in Southeast Bengal* (1992), 8.

9.   Collapse of textile trade: Taylor, *A Sketch of the Topography & Statistics of Dacca* (1840), 364–6. The British author was Horace Hayman Wilson, quoted in Dutt's *Economic History of India* (1906), 263.

9.   Effects in Dacca: Taylor, *A Sketch of the Topography & Statistics of Dacca* (1840), 366.

10.   Effects in Noakhali: Bhattacharya and Chaudhuri, 'Regional Economy' (1983), 282; Hunter, *A Statistical Account of Bengal*, vi (1876), 288, 321.

10–11. The collector: Collector to Commissioner of Revenue, Chittagong, 1 Apr. 1861 and 11 Mar. 1864, in Noma and Chakraborty, eds, *Agricultural and Rural Development in Bangladesh* (1990), 45–6, 52.

11.   Salt production: Beveridge, *The District of Bakarganj* (1876), 33–6; *Report of the Commissioner* (1856), 144–6; Serajuddin, 'The Salt Monopoly of the East India Company's Government in Bengal' (1978), 304–322; Barui, *The Salt Industry of Bengal* (1985), 14–27.

11.   Preventive stations: *Report of the Commissioner* (1856), 167–75; appx C, no. 6, 1856, 509; Buchanan, *Francis Buchanan in Southeast Bengal* (1992), 41–8.

12.   Reasons for tax: *Report of the Commissioner* (1856), 174–84; appx H, no. 1, 1836, 625–6; appx E, no. 8, 1835, 545–63; appx D, no. 2, 1832, 523–4; appx J, no. 6, 1853, 658–62; *Report from the Select Committee* (1871), Minutes of Evidence, 174.

12.   Exploitation of salt-makers: Westland, *A Report on the District of Jessore* (1871), 84–91; Beveridge, *The District of Bakarganj* (1876), 185, 319–20.

12–13. Dangers of salt-making: *Report of the Commissioner* (1856), appx C, no. 2, 1856, 474–83; *Report from the Select Committee* (1836), 56–7.

13.   'Law of chances': *Report of the Commissioner* (1856), appx R, no. 2, 1836, 732.

13.   Revenue interests: Beveridge, *The District of Bakarganj* (1876), 169–70.

13–14. Commercial interests: *Report of the Commissioner* (1856), 1–5; appx D, no. 2, 1832, 523–4; appx E, no. 8, 1835, 545–63.

14.   Employment of salt-makers: Webster, *Noakhali* (1911), 68; *Report from the Select Committee* (1836), appx, no. 48, 1835, 138–43; *Report of the Commissioner* (1856), 167–75; Hunter, *A Statistical Account of Bengal*, vi (1876), 256; *Report from the Select Committee* (1871), Minutes of Evidence, 144.

15.   Land use: Beveridge, *The District of Bakarganj* (1876), 292.

15.   Prevention: *Report of the Commissioner* (1856), appx C, no. 4, 1856, 499–504; Superintendent of Salt Chaukis, Bullooah to Controller of Govt Salt Chaukis, Calcutta, 14 Oct. 1857, CSCR, WBSA, 13–27.

15–16. Price: *Report of the Commissioner* (1856), 174–84; appx H, no. 1, 1836, 625–6; *Report from the Select Committee* (1871), Minutes of Evidence, 146.

16–17. Permanent Settlement: Bose, *Peasant Labour and Colonial Capital* (1993), 112–13; Palit, *Tensions in Bengal Rural Society* (1975), 26.

17.   Intention to resume: Pargiter, *A Revenue History of the Sundarbans* (1934), 9; Phillips, *The Law Relating to the Land Tenures of Lower Bengal* (1876), 463–4; Bose, *Peasant Labour and Colonial Capital* (1993), 112–13.

17.   Resumption proceedings: Thompson, *Final Report* (1919), 68; Beveridge, *The District of Bakarganj* (1876), 321.

17–18. Alluvion and Diluvion Regulation: 'The Bengal Alluvion and Diluvion Regulation', 1825; Sen, *Final Report* (1939), 12–13.

18.   Implications for landowners: Beveridge, *The District of Bakarganj* (1876), 61.

18.   Sandwip: Sen, *Final Report* (1939), 12–13.

18.   Dakhin Shahbazpur: Beveridge, *The District of Bakarganj* (1876), 135, 140, 181–3; Basu, *Survey and Settlement of the Dakhin Shahbazpur Estates* (1896), 8.

18–19. 'A natural consequence': Beveridge, *The District of Bakarganj* (1876), 181.

19.   Benefits to government: Thompson, *Final Report* (1919), 71; Palit, *Tensions in Bengal Rural Society* (1975), 28, 38, 59; Beveridge, *The District of Bakarganj* (1876), 186–7; Hunter, *A Statistical Account of Bengal*, vi (1876), 239.

19–20. Zamindars: Collector to Commissioner of Revenue, Chittagong, 9 Sept. 1863, in Noma and Chakraborty, eds, *Agricultural and Rural Development in Bangladesh* (1990), 80–1; Hunter, *A Statistical Account of Bengal*, vi (1876), 319.

20.   Ill health: Collector to Commissioner of Revenue, Chittagong, 9

Sept. 1863, in Noma and Chakraborty, eds, *Agricultural and Rural Development in Bangladesh* (1990), 80–1; Gastrell, *Geographical and Statistical Report* (1868), 4; Hunter, *A Statistical Account of Bengal*, vi (1876), 346–7.

20.   Religious impurity: Webster, *Noakhali* (1911), 3, 14, 19, 25.

21.   Government officials: Dy Collector to Collector, 14 Aug. 1867, in Noma and Chakraborty, eds, *Agricultural and Rural Development in Bangladesh* (1990), 171–3. Chittagong was another notorious hardship posting. 'A sink of iniquity', one of its commissioners called it, 'full of the scum of various nations ... it is deadly unhealthy, isolated from the rest of India, and the work is not only heavy but of a peculiarly troublesome and intricate kind. The dirt, the noxious vermin, and the smells are unique.' Beames, *Memoirs of a Bengal Civilian* (1961), 276.

21.   Cultivators' views: Thompson, *Final Report* (1919), 21–2.

21.   Herdsmen: Hunter, *A Statistical Account of Bengal*, vi (1876), 258, 274.

22.   Preparing the land: Sen, *Final Report* (1939), 3, 17; Hunter, *A Statistical Account of Bengal*, vi (1876), 302–3; Webster, *Noakhali* (1911), 80–1; Thompson, *Final Report* (1919), 5.

22.   Population pressure: Bose, *Peasant Labour and Colonial Capital* (1993), 14–15.

23.   Noakhali population 1798–1803: Thompson, *Final Report* (1919), 24; Buchanan, *Francis Buchanan in Southeast Bengal* (1992), 12; 'Extract from Mr. R. Knox's Field Book', 1803, NAI, passim.

23.   Noakhali population 1872–1876: Thompson, *Final Report* (1919), 22; Hunter, *A Statistical Account of Bengal*, vi (1876), 301; Bose, *Peasant Labour and Colonial Capital* (1993), 23.

23–4.   Rents and tenure: Bose, *Peasant Labour and Colonial Capital* (1993), 21; 'Extract from Mr. R. Knox's Field Book', 1803, NAI, 46, 61; Beveridge, *The District of Bakarganj* (1876), 292; Hunter, *A Statistical Account of Bengal*, vi (1876), 314–15.

24.   Displacement: Beveridge, *The District of Bakarganj* (1876), 20–2.

24–6.   Kuber's story: Bandyopadhyay, *The Boatman of the Padma* (2012), 27, 43, 97–9, 112–16.

26. Lakhipur: Rennell, *Memoir of a Map of Hindoostan* (1793), 350–1.

26–7. Storms and embankments: Blanford, 'Catalogue of the Recorded Cyclones in the Bay of Bengal' (1877), 328–38; Hunter, *A Statistical Account of Bengal*, vi (1876), 254, 317; Manager of Paikpara Estate to Collector, 11 Nov. 1867, and Dy Magistrate to Magistrate, 27 Nov. 1867, in Noma and Chakraborty, eds, *Agricultural and Rural Development in Bangladesh* (1990), 4–5, 8–12.

27. Responsibility for embankments: Harrison, *The Bengal Embankment Manual* (1875), 4; Hunter, *A Statistical Account of Bengal*, vi (1876), 254.

27. Bamni flooded: Extracts from the Diary of the Superintendent of Police, 18, 19, and 20 May 1869, in Noma and Chakraborty, eds, *Agricultural and Rural Development in Bangladesh* (1990), 26.

27–8. Reginald Porch: Porch is quoted in Hunter, *A Statistical Account of Bengal*, vi (1876), 317–18.

28. Loss of life: Blanford, 'Catalogue of the Recorded Cyclones in the Bay of Bengal' (1877), 332, 337.

2. THE FOREST

29. The Sundarbans: Rennell, *Memoir of a Map of Hindoostan* (1793), 339; Pogson, *Captain Pogson's Narrative* (1831), 15–16.

29–30. Charles Grant: Grant, *Observations on the State of Society* (1797), i, 71, 153; Arnold, 'Agriculture and "Improvement" in Early Colonial India' (2005), 505–25.

30. Permanent Settlement: Guha, *A Rule of Property for Bengal* (2016), 219–228; Metcalf, *Ideologies of the Raj* (1995), 20–1.

30. William Carey: Carey, 'Prospectus of an Agricultural and Horticultural Society' (1821), 254–6.

31. Murshid Quli and Mir Kasim: Karim, *Murshid Quli Khan and His Times* (1963), 74–93; Marshall, *Bengal: The British Bridgehead* (1987), 59, 140–2.

31. Company's demands: Marshall, *Bengal: The British Bridgehead* (1987), 140–2.

31–2. Henckell's plan: Westland, *A Report on the District of Jessore* (1871), 135–7; Pargiter, *A Revenue History of the Sundarbans* (1934), 1–4.

32.   Problems: Westland, *A Report on the District of Jessore* (1871), 137–9.

32–3.   1814 to 1828: Pargiter, *A Revenue History of the Sundarbans* (1934), 6–23.

33.   Dampier's proceedings: Pargiter, *A Revenue History of the Sundarbans* (1934), 23–40; Beveridge, *The District of Bakarganj* (1876), 139.

33–4.   Pressures of Permanent Settlement: Islam, *The Permanent Settlement in Bengal* (1979), 252–4; Beveridge, *The District of Bakarganj* (1876), 60–1; Raychaudhuri, 'Permanent Settlement in Operation' (1969), 165–6.

34.   Advantages of temporary settlement: 'Temporary Settlement', in Islam, ed., *Banglapedia* (2006).

34–5.   Government grants: Pargiter, *A Revenue History of the Sundarbans* (1934), 35–6, 56–7.

35.   Henry Piddington: Piddington, *The Sailor's Horn-Book for the Law of Storms* (1848), 7–8; *A Letter to the Most Noble James Andrew* (1853), 18–20.

35–6.   Terms relaxed: Pargiter, *A Revenue History of the Sundarbans* (1934), 93; Dalhousie is quoted in *The Mutlah as an Auxiliary Port to Calcutta* (1858), 42–3.

36.   Physical geography: Hunter, *A Statistical Account of Bengal*, i (1875), 287.

36–7.   Deforestation in Bakarganj: Pellew, 'Physical Characteristics of Backergunge' (1864), 202–3; Gastrell, *Geographical and Statistical Report* (1868), 25; Beverley, *Report on the Census of Bengal* (1872), appx B, x–xii.

37.   Embankments: Pogson, *Captain Pogson's Narrative* (1831), 35.

37–8.   Conservation proposal: Guha, 'State Forestry and Social Conflict' (1989), 144–5; Ascoli, *A Revenue History of the Sundarbans* (1921), 55–6.

38.   Exhaustion and reservation: Ascoli, *A Revenue History of the Sundarbans* (1921), 56–7. Temple is quoted on 14–15.

39.   Protective role: Gastrell and Blanford, *Report on the Calcutta Cyclone* (1866); Gastrell, *Geographical and Statistical Report* (1868), 25; Westland, *A Report on the District of Jessore* (1871), 234; Hunter, *A Statistical Account of Bengal*, i (1875), 289.

39–40. An exception: Gastrell, *Geographical and Statistical Report* (1868), 28–9.

40. Woodcutters: Pargiter, 'Cameos of Indian Districts' (1889), 298–9; Hunter, *A Statistical Account of Bengal*, i (1875), 304, 312; Westland, *A Report on the District of Jessore* (1871), 240–3; Beveridge, *The District of Bakarganj* (1876), 287–8.

40. Maghs: Sunder, *The Mughs of the Sundarbans* (1903), 1–7; Pargiter, 'Cameos of Indian Districts' (1889), 300; Hunter, *A Statistical Account of Bengal*, i (1875), 319–20; Beveridge, *The District of Bakarganj* (1876), 163–9.

40–1. Difficulties of forest clearance: Westland, *A Report on the District of Jessore* (1871), 226–8; Pargiter, 'Cameos of Indian Districts' (1889), 300.

41. Cultivation: Hunter, *A Statistical Account of Bengal*, i (1875), 324; Beveridge, *The District of Bakarganj* (1876), 278–80; Jack, *Final Report* (1915), 25.

41–2. Floods and rains: Jack, *Final Report* (1915), 22–5; Banerjee, *Agricultural Sayings in Bengal* (1914), 1–2, 18–19.

42. 'The few cases of poverty': Hunter, *A Statistical Account of Bengal*, i (1875), 322.

42. Origins of subdivided tenure: Jack, *Final Report* (1915), 43–6.

42–3. Lengthening tenure chain: Jack, *Final Report* (1915), 46–7; Eaton, *The Rise of Islam and the Bengal Frontier* (1994), 220–1; Hunter, *A Statistical Account of Bengal*, v (1875), 369–70. An unusually energetic zamindar might organise a colony of cultivators himself, tempting them with cash advances, food, cattle, and even houses—'somewhat as the New Zealand Government acts with emigrants'. Beveridge, *The District of Bakarganj* (1876), 203.

43. Absentees: Beveridge, *The District of Bakarganj* (1876), 192; Jack, *Final Report* (1915), 62, 66, 113.

43–4. Dampier's letter: Dampier to Board of Revenue, 10 Sept. 1832, quoted in Jack, *Final Report* (1915), 118–19.

44–5. Dampier's settlements: Pargiter, *A Revenue History of the Sundarbans* (1934), 40.

45. Official and actual rates of rent: Islam, *Bengal Land Tenure* (1988),

67; Hunter, *A Statistical Account of Bengal*, v (1875), 209–11; Nakazato, *Agrarian System in Eastern Bengal* (1994), 251–3.

45.   Hunter's figures: Dutt, *Open Letters to Lord Curzon* (1900), 61–2; Bose, *Peasant Labour and Colonial Capital* (1993), 120; Nakazato, *Agrarian System in Eastern Bengal* (1994), 258; Hunter, *A Statistical Account of Bengal*, v (1875), 204–5, 209–11; i (1875), 336.

45–6.   Varieties of abwab: Jack, *Final Report* (1915), 79; Palit, *Tensions in Bengal Rural Society* (1975), 80–1.

46.   Personal power: Jack, *Final Report* (1915), 83; Raychaudhuri, 'Permanent Settlement in Operation' (1969), 172.

46–7.   Means of coercion: Palit, *Tensions in Bengal Rural Society* (1975), 19; Jack, *Final Report* (1915), 83–4; Beames, *Memoirs of a Bengal Civilian* (1961), 137.

47.   Rent Act: Bose, *Peasant Labour and Colonial Capital* (1993), 119.

47.   Access to courts: Jack, *Final Report* (1915), 99; Beveridge, *The District of Bakarganj* (1876), 367; Palit, *Tensions in Bengal Rural Society* (1975), 81.

47–8.   Zamindar's diary: Quoted in Jack, *Final Report* (1915), 81–2.

48–9.   Desertion: Dy Collector to Commissioner of Sundarbans, 15 Oct. 1851, PCSR, WBSA, folder 29.

49.   Transferring allegiance: Beveridge, *The District of Bakarganj* (1876), 200–2.

49.   Faraizis: Ahmed, *The Bengal Muslims* (1981), 39–41; Wise, *Notes on the Races, Castes, and Trades* (1883), 24.

3. THE CYCLONE

51–3.   Path of cyclone: Elliott, *Report of the Vizagapatam and Backergunge Cyclones* (1877), 88, 94, 108–12, 116, 120–2, 133–6, 141, 158–62.

53.   Effects in Dacca: Peacock to Secy to GoB, 4 Nov. 1876, 55.

53.   Effects in Barisal: Barton to Peacock, 1 Nov. 1876, 57–8. The most important sources for the effects of the cyclone in Bakarganj, and the government's response to it, are the letters exchanged between Barton and Peacock. Barton's letters often include enclosures from the lower district officials, most of whom were Bengalis.

The letters are reprinted in the volumes of official proceedings held at the West Bengal State Archives in Calcutta.

54. Tajammal Ali: Barton to Peacock, 2 Nov. 1876, 58–9.

54–5. Deenanath Sarkar: Statement of Deena Nath Sarkar, 3 Nov. 1876, 61–2.

55–6. Umacharan Banerjee: Barton to Peacock, 6 Feb. 1877 [Mar. 1877], 76–7.

56. Patuakhali officials: Barton to Peacock, 4 Nov. 1876, 109–10.

56. Relief on 2 November: Barton to Peacock, 2 Nov. 1876, 58–9.

57. Relief on 3 November: Barton to Peacock, 3 Nov. 1876, 60–1.

57. 'A dereliction of duty': Barton to Peacock, 2 Nov. 1876, 58–9.

57. Logistical difficulties: Barton to Peacock, 3 Nov. 1876, 60–1.

57–8. Harris's report: Harris to Barton, 4 Nov. 1876, 78–9; Harris to Barton, 7 Nov 1876, 95–6.

58. Barton's relief plan: Barton to Peacock, 4 Nov. 1876, 77–8.

58–9. Stress: Barton to Peacock, 4 Nov. 1876, 77–8.

59–60. Kerry's report: Kerry to Barton, 5 & 6 Nov. 1876, 89–90.

60. Profiteering: Barton to Peacock, 3 Nov. 1876, 60–1; Barton to Peacock, 10 Nov. 1876, 97.

60. Indian civil service: Gilmour, *The Ruling Caste* (2005), 47–50.

61. Peacock's response: Peacock to Secy to GoB, 6 Nov. 1876, 71–2; Peacock to Secy to GoB, 7 Nov. 1876, 73–4; Peacock to Secy to GoB, 8 Nov. 1876, 77.

61. Lyall's opinion: Memo by Lyall, 11 Nov. 1876, 101.

62. Effects in Sudharam: Porch to Smith, 1 Nov. 1876, 93–4.

62. Officials sent out: Porch to Supt of Police, 2 Nov. 1876, NDR 80, 126; Porch to Dutt, Ghose, and Naib of Bhulua, 3 Nov. 1876, NDR 80, 129.

63. Bore and storm-wave: Elliott, *Report of the Vizagapatam and Backergunge Cyclones* (1877), 158–80.

64. Messages to Calcutta and Dacca: Porch to Secy to GoB, 5 Nov. 1876, 71; Porch to Secy to GoB, 6 Nov. 1876, 56.

64. Kalinath Bose: Porch to Bose and Majumder, 3 Nov. 1876, NDR 80, 133–4; Porch to Bose, 5 Nov. 1876, NDR 80, 145.

64–5. Alexander Smith: Smith to Secy to GoB, 3 Nov. 1876, 83.

65–6.   John Veasey: Veasey to Smith, 2 Nov. 1876, 83–4; Veasey to Smith, 4 Nov. 1876, 107–8; Veasey to Smith, 8 Nov. 1876, 177–8; *Hindoo Patriot*, 13 Nov. and 27 Nov. 1876.

66.   Porch's instructions: Porch to Sarkar, 5 Nov. 1876, NDR 80, 143–4.

67–8.   Personnel shortage: Barton to Peacock, 3 Nov. 1876, 63; Harris to Barton, 4 Nov. 1876, 78–9; Porch to Smith, 18 Nov. 1876, NDR 81, 70–2; Bose to Smith, 4 Dec. 1876, NDR 81, 85.

68.   Property loss: Harris to Barton, 4 Nov. 1876, 78–9.

68.   Government records: Harris to Barton, 7 Nov. 1876, 98–9; Tajammal Ali to Barton, 4 Nov. 1876, 104–5.

68–9.   Bakarganj law and order: Harris to Barton, 4 Nov. 1876, 78–9; Harris to Barton, 7 Nov. 1876, 87; Kerry to Barton, 5 & 6 Nov. 1876, 89–90.

69.   Chittagong and Noakhali: Veasey to Smith, 2 Nov. 1876, 83–4; Veasey to Smith, 6 Nov. 1876, 176–7; Porch to Smith, 7 Nov. 1876, 135–6.

69.   Predisposition to crime: The magistrate is quoted in Beveridge, *The District of Bakarganj* (1876), 417; Parker is quoted in the same source, 443–4. See also Hunter, *A Statistical Account of Bengal*, vi (1876), 335.

69–70.   Administrative developments: Beveridge, *The District of Bakarganj* (1876), 326, 347; Hunter, *A Statistical Account of Bengal*, vi (1876), 330–1.

70.   Strengthening police: Harris to Barton, 4 Nov. 1876, 78–9; Harris to Barton, 7 Nov. 1876, 87; Veasey to Smith, 4 Nov. 1876, 107–8; Porch to Supt of Police, 4 Nov. 1876, NDR 80, 134.

70.   Looting: Magistrate to Commissioner of Revenue, 9 Apr. 1872, in Noma and Chakraborty, eds, *Agricultural and Rural Development in Bangladesh* (1990), 142; Bose to Smith, 25 Nov. 1876, NDR 81, 75; Smith to Secy to General Dept, 23 Nov. 1876 [Dec. 1876], 227–9; Kerry to Barton, 7 Nov. 1876, 98; Pellew to Porch, 8 Dec. 1876 [Jan 1877], 9–11.

71.   Inhabitants of Barisal: Beveridge, *The District of Bakarganj* (1876), 11, 367–71.

71.   Housing in Barisal: Barton to Peacock, 1 Nov. 1876, 57–8.

72.   Noakhali: Porch to Smith, 1 Nov. 1876, 93–4.

72.   Chittagong: Hunter, *A Statistical Account of Bengal*, vi (1876), 150–1; Veasey to Smith, 2 Nov. 1876, 83–4; Smith to Secy to GoB, 4 Nov. 1876, 76; *Bengal Times*, 8 Nov. 1876.

72.   Beyond the towns: Beveridge, *The District of Bakarganj* (1876), 136; Barton to Peacock, 3 Nov. 1876, 76.

72–3.   Forest clearings and chars: Minute by Temple, 21 Nov. 1876, 151–7; Jack, *Final Report* (1915), 120.

73.   Trees as protection: Sen and Sen to Barton, 3 Jan. 1877 [Feb. 1877], 45–55; Ascoli, *A Revenue History of the Sundarbans* (1921), 71.

73–4.   Magh settlements: Gupta to Barton, 22 Nov. 1876, 199–200; Wight, 'Report on Chapli', 14 July 1873, SDP/IS, WBSA, 23–8.

74.   Boatmen and fishermen: Barton to Peacock, 1 Nov. 1876, 57–8; Supt of Police to Magistrate of Chittagong, 14 Feb. 1877 [Apr. 1877], 107–8.

74.   Landlords and agents: Harris to Barton, 4. Nov 1876, 78–9; Beveridge, *The District of Bakarganj* (1876), 193; *Bengal Times*, 11 Nov. 1876.

75.   Children and old people: Porch to Smith, 8 Nov. 1876, 180; Smith to Secy to General Department, 23 Nov. 1876 [Dec 1876], 213–17; Gupta to Barton, 22 Nov. 1876, 133; Sen and Sen to Barton, 3 Jan. 1877 [Feb. 1877], 45–55; Barton to Peacock, 2 Nov. 1876, 58.

75.   Women in Bakarganj and Noakhali: Beveridge, *The District of Bakarganj* (1876), 224–8, 283–4; Eaton, *The Rise of Islam and the Bengal Frontier* (1994), 297–301. Reilly is quoted in Hunter, *A Statistical Account of Bengal*, v (1875), 231.

76.   Death toll among women: Barton to Peacock, 4 Nov. 1876, 75; Porch to Smith, 8 Nov. 1876, 180; Gupta to Barton, 22 Nov. 1876, 133; Sen and Sen to Barton, 3 Jan. 1877 [Feb. 1877], 45–55; Beveridge, *The District of Bakarganj* (1876), 271.

76.   Reasons: Gupta to Barton, 22 Nov. 1876, 133; Begum, 'Women in Environmental Disasters' (1993), 34; Porch to Smith, 1 Nov. 1876, 93–4.

76. Nabin Sen: Sen is quoted in the second volume of Nirad Chaudhuri's autobiography, *Thy Hand, Great Anarch!* (1990), 214.

4. THE RESPONSE

79. Temple's launch: Temple, *The Story of My Life*, i (1896), 257–9.
79–80. Temple in Noakhali: Porch to Smith, 8 Nov. 1876, 180.
80. 'No flattery was too gross': Beames, *Memoirs of a Bengal Civilian* (1961), 236, 238–40. Beames was the collector of Cuttack, in Orissa, at the time of Temple's visit in 1874. On the last night of the visit, after Temple had retired and more champagne had been brought in, he gave a speech parodying the lieutenant governor. 'Of course I was excited, and the long pent-up feeling of disgust at the vanity and self-glorification of this windbag was irrepressible. I mimicked his manner, I satirized his past career ... all sorts of smart things leapt to my lips.' Unfortunately for Beames, one of Temple's staff was hiding behind a curtain and reported the performance to the lieutenant governor. This indiscretion, Beames believed, was 'the real cause of my ill-success in the later part of my career'.
80. Tours by 'great men': Beames, *Memoirs of a Bengal Civilian* (1961), 237–8.
80–1. Inspection and conclusions: Minute by Temple, 21 Nov. 1876, 151–7.
81. Rules: Temple to Peacock, [12 Nov. 1876], 112–13.
81–3. Famine of 1873–74: Campbell, *Memoirs of My Indian Career*, ii (1893), 320–4, 330; Beames, *Memoirs of a Bengal Civilian* (1961), 231–2; Ambirajan, *Classical Political Economy* (1978), 86–92.
83. The critics: *The Economist*, 4 July 1874, 801–2.
83–4. The pamphlet: *The Black Pamphlet of Calcutta* (1876), iv, viii, 3, 7. This wasn't the last time O'Donnell would launch an abusive attack on his superiors, but none of his subsequent polemics would have the deadly effect of the 'Black Pamphlet'. See Gilmour, *The Ruling Caste* (2005), 141–5.
84. Temple's career: Temple, *The Story of My Life*, i (1896), v, 284–5.

84–5.   Temple's minute: Temple, *The Story of My Life*, i (1896), x, 255; Minute by Temple, 21 Nov. 1876, 151–7.

85.   Free-market relief: Ambirajan, *Classical Political Economy* (1978), 9–17, 99–100.

86.   Salvaging food: Smith to Secy to General Dept, 23 Nov. 1876 [Dec. 1876], 213–17; *Hindoo Patriot*, 27 Nov. 1876.

86–7.   Crop expectations: Elliott, *Report of the Vizagapatam and Backergunge Cyclones* (1877), 163; Minute by Temple, 21 Nov. 1876, 151–7; Gupta to Barton, 22 Nov. 1876, 199–200.

87.   Labour shortage: Gupta to Barton, 22 Nov. 1876, 199–200.

87–8.   Crop damage: Smith to Secy to General Dept, 23 Nov. 1876 [Dec. 1876], 213–17.

88.   Petitions for relief: Veasey to Smith, 8 Nov. 1876, 177–8; *Hindoo Patriot*, 27 Nov. 1876.

88.   Betel nuts: Minute by Temple, 21 Nov. 1876, 151–7; Beveridge, *The District of Bakarganj* (1876), 285–6; Jack, *Final Report* (1915), 36.

88–9.   Ghost cyclone: Gupta to Barton, 24 Nov. 1876, 198; *Friend of India*, 2 Dec. 1876; Bose to Smith, 25 Nov. 1876, NDR 81, 74–5.

89.   Effects: Sen and Sen to Barton, 3 Jan. 1877 [Feb. 1877], 45–55; Barton to Peacock, 7 Jan. 1877 [Feb. 1877], 41–5; Beveridge, *The District of Bakarganj* (1876), 279; Jack, *Final Report* (1915), 29.

89–90.   Char Bhuta: Sen and Sen to Barton, 3 Jan. 1877 [Feb. 1877], 45–55.

90.   Loss of cattle and ploughs: Peacock to Secy to GoB, 19 Nov. 1876, 189–95; Gupta to Barton, 22 Nov. 1876, 199–200; Smith to Secy to General Dept, 23 Nov. 1876 [Dec. 1876], 213–17.

90.   Homesteads: Smith to Secy to GoB, 12 Nov. 1876, 175–6; Junior Secy to GoB to Smith, 27 Nov. 1876, 183.

90–1.   Polluted water: Veasey to Smith, 8 Nov. 1876, 177–8; Smith to Secy to GoB, 12 Nov. 1876, 175–6; Minute by Temple, 21 Nov. 1876, 151–7.

91–2.   End of relief in Noakhali: Porch to Smith, 10 Nov. 1876, 181; Porch to Captain of the *Star of Dacca*, 13 Nov. 1876, NDR 80, 173–4; Porch to Sen, 14 Nov. 1876, NDR 80, 179–80; Porch to

Sub-Dy Magistrate, 15 Nov. 1876, NDR 80, 182–3; Porch to Sen, [15 or 16 Nov. 1876], NDR 80, 192–4; Porch to Sarkar, [10 or 11 Nov. 1876], NDR 80, 164–7.

92. Chittagong: Smith to Secy to GoB, 12 Nov. 1876, 175–6.

92. Pellew to Sandwip and Hatia: *The Bengalee*, 6 Jan. 1877; Minute by Temple, 19 Nov. 1876, 143–4.

92–3. Peacock to Bakarganj: Peacock to Secy to GoB, 19 Nov. 1876, 189–95.

93–4. Number of deaths: Minute by Temple, 21 Nov. 1876, 151–7.

94. Ananda Sen: Harris to Barton, 23 Nov. 1876, 198–9.

94. Barton reprimanded: Secy to GoB to Peacock, 16 Nov. 1876, 131; *The Bengalee*, 18 Nov. 1876.

95. Barton's explanation: Barton to Peacock, 20 Nov. 1876 [Dec. 1876], 231–2.

95. Final accounts: Barton to Peacock, 6 Feb. 1877 [Mar. 1877], 83–4; *The Bengalee*, 10 Mar. 1877; Memo by Lowis, 18 Apr. 1877, FDP/M [May 1877], 143–4.

95–6. Spending on police: Temple to Peacock, [12 Nov. 1876], 112–3; Minute by Temple, 21 Nov. 1876, 151–7; Memo by Lowis, 18 Apr. 1877, FDP/M [May 1877], 143–4.

96–7. Zamindars' response: Mahomed to Barton, 4 Nov. 1876, 102–3; Pellew to Porch, 8 Dec. 1876 [Jan. 1877], 9–11; Porch to Lowis, 3 Apr. 1877, NDR 81, 179–85; *Hindoo Patriot*, 11 Dec. 1876; *Soma Prakash*, 6 Nov. 1876, RNN.

97. Baptists in Bakarganj: Annual Report for 1875–6, ALA, 57–8; *Missionary Herald*, Jan. 1874, 6; Sept. 1874, 166; May 1876, 94; Beveridge, *The District of Bakarganj* (1876), 247, 260–3.

97–8. Difficulties of missionary work: Annual Report for 1877–8, ALA, 15–16; *Missionary Herald*, Oct. 1875, 190–2; Jan. 1876, 4; Feb. 1876, 29–31; Mar. 1876, 53–4.

98. Response to Bengal famine: *Missionary Herald*, Jan. 1874, 6; Mar. 1874, 41–2; Apr. 1874, 67–8; May 1874, 91–2; May 1875, 94–5.

98. Experience of cyclone: *Missionary Herald*, Jan. 1877, 7–8.

98–9. Relief mission: *Missionary Herald*, Jan. 1877, 3–7.

99. Prayer and evangelism: *Missionary Herald*, Jan. 1877, 19; May 1877, 97; May 1874, 91–2; Jan. 1877, 6–7.

99.   Missionary contribution: Annual Report for 1876–7, ALA, 230–1; *Missionary Herald*, May 1877, 97.

99–100. Appeals for relief: The *Indian Daily News* is quoted in the *Missionary Herald*, Jan. 1877, 3–5; *Hindoo Patriot*, 13 Nov. and 20 Nov. 1876.

100.   Calcutta's contributions: Barton to Peacock, 4 Jan. 1877, 26; Peacock to Secy to GoB, 29 Nov. 1876 [Dec. 1876], 225; Peacock to Secy to Financial Dept, 7 Apr. 1877, 138–9; *Hindoo Patriot*, 11 Dec. 1876; Beveridge, *The District of Bakarganj* (1876), 130–1.

100–1. An astonishing suggestion: Barton to Peacock, 4 Jan. 1877, 26; Peacock to Secy to Financial Dept, 15 Jan. 1877, 26; Junior Secy to GoB to Peacock, 23 Jan. 1877, 26–7.

101.   1867 subscriptions: Correspondence regarding action taken for the relief of distress caused by a cyclone, Nov.–Dec. 1867, L/PJ 3/1103 No. 20, IOR; Bengal special narrative on the hurricane of 1st and 2nd November 1867, Nov.–Dec. 1867, L/PJ 3/1103 No. 27, IOR; *Report of the Committee of the Cyclone Relief Fund of 1867* (1868), 44.

102.   First news: *The Bengalee*, 11 Nov. and 18 Nov. 1876.

102–3. Criticisms of durbar: *The Bengalee*, 18 Nov., 25 Nov., and 9 Dec. 1876; *Soma Prakash*, 6 Nov. 1876, RNN; *Bharat Mihir*, 7 Dec. 1876, RNN; *Bishwa Suhrid*, 6 Dec. 1876, RNN.

103–4. General criticisms: *The Bengalee*, 9 Dec. 1876 and 6 Jan. 1877.

104.   British-owned papers: *Friend of India*, 30 Dec. 1876.

104–6. Critical responses to Temple's minute: *Amrita Bazar Patrika*, 9 Nov. and 28 Dec. 1876; *The Bengalee*, 2 Dec. 1876; *Bharat Mihir*, 7 Dec. 1876, RNN; *Bishwa Suhrid*, 13 Dec. 1876, RNN; *Friend of India*, 2 Dec. 1876.

106–7. An exception: *Hindoo Patriot*, 13 Nov., 20 Nov., and 27 Nov. 1876.

107.   Criticism of Bengalis: *Amrita Bazar Patrika*, 16 Nov. and 28 Dec. 1876.

107–8. The durbar: *The Bengalee*, 30 Dec. 1876 and 6 Jan. 1877; Secy to Government of India to Secy to GoB, 24 Nov. 1876, 187–8;

Temple, *The Story of My Life*, i (1896), 289; [O'Donnell], *The Black Pamphlet of Calcutta* (1876), v.

108. Verdict on Temple's departure: *Hindu Hitoishini*, 16 Dec. 1876, RNN.

5. THE EPIDEMIC

109. Sitakund hills: Hunter, *A Statistical Account of Bengal*, vi (1876), 232–3; O'Malley, *Chittagong* (1908), 189–90.

109–10. Pilgrims: Veasey to Smith, 2 Nov. 1876, 83–4; Smith to Secy to General Dept, 23 Nov. 1876 [Dec. 1876], 213–17; Supt of Police to Magistrate of Chittagong, 14 Feb. 1877 [Apr. 1877], 107–8.

110. Pargiter: Veasey to Smith, 6 Nov. 1876, 176–7; Veasey to Smith, 8 Nov. 1876, 177–8; Smith to Secy to General Dept, 23 Nov. 1876 [Dec. 1876], 213–17.

110. Noakhali: Porch to Secy to GoB, 5 Nov. 1876, 71; Porch to Smith, 10 Nov. 1876, 181.

110. Bakarganj and Temple: Barton to Peacock, 16 Mar. 1877 [Apr. 1877], 120–2; Minute by Temple, 21 Nov. 1876, 151–7.

111. 1817 epidemic: Westland, *A Report on the District of Jessore* (1871), 178–83.

111. Symptoms: Murray, *Report on the Treatment of Epidemic Cholera* (1869), 1–2.

111–12. Theories: Murray, *Report on the Treatment of Epidemic Cholera* (1869), 2–3; Macnamara, *A History of Asiatic Cholera* (1876), v–x; Bellew, *Cholera in India, 1862–1881* (1884), 16–17, 28, 51, 109; Arnold, 'Cholera and Colonialism in British India' (1986), 143–5; Harrison, *Public Health in British India* (1994), 99–109.

112. Consensus: Bellew, *Cholera in India* (1884), 135–6; Murray, *Report on the Treatment of Epidemic Cholera* (1869), 3.

112–13. Dead bodies: Chaudhuri to Barton, 7 Nov. 1876, 109–10; Kerry to Barton, 5 & 6 Nov. 1876, 89–90; *Bengal Times*, 23 Dec. 1876; Lowis to Secy to Financial Dept, 27 Apr. 1877, FDP/M [May 1877], 3–7; *Hindoo Patriot*, 27 Nov. 1876.

113–14. Religious and caste prejudices: Veasey to Smith, 4 Nov. 1876, 107–8; Harris to Barton, 4 Nov. 1876, 78–9; Harris to Barton, 7 Nov.

1876, 87. See also Ahmed, *The Bengal Muslims* (1981), 18–20, and Wise, *Notes on the Races, Castes, and Trades* (1883), 42–3.

114.   Practical difficulties: Gupta to Barton, 10 Nov. 1876, 133.

114.   Government doctors: Arnold, *Science, Technology and Medicine* (2004), 61–5.

115.   Spread of disease: Lowis to Secy to Financial Dept, 27 Apr. 1877, FDP/M [May 1877], 3–7.

115.   Coates' plan: Lowis to Secy to Financial Dept, 27 Apr. 1877, FDP/M [May 1877], 3–7.

115.   Steamer refused: Lowis to Secy to GoB, 12 Dec. 1876, 241; Junior Secy to GoB to Lowis, 13 Dec. 1876, 233.

115–16. Responsibility for public health: Harrison, *Public Health in British India* (1994), 116; Arnold, *Science, Technology and Medicine* (2004), 58.

116.   Noakhali medical facilities: Hunter, *A Statistical Account of Bengal*, vi (1876), 349–50; Lowis to Secy to Financial Dept, 27 Apr. 1877, FDP/M [May 1877], 3–7; Porch to Lehuraux, Estate of Alfred Courjon, 30 July 1877, NDR 84, 255–6.

116–17. Lyons' recommendations: Porch to Supt of Police, 10 Nov. 1876, NDR 80, 162–3; Lowis to Secy to Financial Dept, 27 Apr. 1877, FDP/M [May 1877], 3–7.

117.   Noakhali developments: Smith to Secy to GoB, 12 Nov. 1876, 175–6; Lowis to Secy to Financial Dept, 27 Apr. 1877, FDP/M [May 1877], 3–7.

117–18. Porch's absence: Eden to Lowis, 12 Jan. 1877, 18; Junior Secy to GoB to Surgeon-General of Indian Medical Dept, 12 Jan. 1877, 18; Lowis to Secy to Financial Dept, 15 Jan. 1877, 28; Junior Secy to GoB to Lowis, 29 Jan. 1877, 28; Porch to Lowis, 23 Feb. 1877 [Mar. 1877], 95–7; Lowis to Secy to Financial Dept, 7 Mar. 1877, 95; Junior Secy to GoB to Lowis, 19 Mar. 1877, 101.

119.   Lyons' medicines: Porch to Secy to GoB, 12 Jan. 1877, 17.

119.   Pills or liquids: Lowis to Secy to Financial Dept, 5 Feb. 1877, 37.

119–20. Homeopathy: 'Mahendralal Sircar', in Islam, ed., *Banglapedia* (2006); *Bharat Sangskarak*, 21 May 1877, RNN; Kidd, *Directions for the Homeopathic Treatment of Cholera* (1866), 5.

NOTES

120. Indian medicine: Beveridge, *The District of Bakarganj* (1876), 258; Wise, *Notes on the Races, Castes, and Trades* (1883), 77–84; Arnold, *Science, Technology and Medicine* (2004), 63–9; Ahmed, *The Bengal Muslims* (1981), 30.

120–1. Treatments: Jameson, *Report on the Epidemick Cholera Morbus* (1820), 243–4.

121. Religious responses: Beveridge, *The District of Bakarganj* (1876), 339, 380; Macnamara, *A History of Asiatic Cholera* (1876), 34–6; Hora, 'Worship of the Deities Ola, Jhola and Bon Bibi in Lower Bengal' (1933), 1–4.

121–2. Preparations in Bakarganj: Cameron to Barton, 14 Mar. 1877 [Apr. 1877], 122–6; Barton to Peacock, 16 Mar. 1877 [Apr. 1877], 120–2.

122. Outbreak: Barton to Peacock, 16 Mar. 1877 [Apr. 1877], 120–2.

122–3. Cameron in Dakhin Shahbazpur: Cameron to Barton, 21 Jan. 1877, 29–30; Cameron to Barton, 14 Mar. 1877 [Apr. 1877], 122–6. There is also a report on the cholera in Bakarganj from a correspondent to the *Indian Daily News*, probably George Kerry, in the *Hindoo Patriot*, 29 Jan. 1877.

123. Reinforcements: Cameron to Barton, 21 Jan. 1877, 29–30.

123. Cameron in Patuakhali: Cameron to Dy Surgeon-General, Dacca, 3 Feb. 1877, 59–63.

124. Placing the blame: Cameron to Barton, 21 Jan. 1877, 29–30; Barton to Peacock, 16 Mar. 1877 [Apr. 1877], 120–2.

124. Situation on Sandwip: Pellew to Porch, 2 Dec. 1876 [Jan. 1877], 4–7; Pellew to Porch, 8 Dec. 1876 [Jan. 1877], 9–11; Smith to Secy to General Dept, 23 Nov. 1876 [Dec. 1876], 213–17.

124–5. Medical assistance: Lowis to Secy to GoB, 11 Dec. 1876, 233.

125. Appalling conditions: Pellew to Porch, 2 Dec. 1876 [Jan. 1877], 4–7.

125–6. No relief: Porch to Pellew, 5 Dec. 1876, NDR 80, 281; Pellew to Porch, 9 Dec. 1876 [Jan. 1877], 11–13; Memo by Lowis, 14 Dec. 1876 [Jan. 1877], 3.

126. Responsibility: Pellew to Porch, 9 Dec. 1876 [Jan. 1877], 11–13.

126–7.   Criticisms of government: *Bharat Mihir*, 7 Dec. 1876, RNN; *Hindoo Patriot*, 20 Nov. and 25 Dec. 1876; *Amrita Bazar Patrika* (Bengali edn), 28 Dec. 1876, RNN.

127–8.   Lack of public interest: *Bharat Sangskarak*, 29 Jan. 1877, RNN; *Hindoo Patriot*, 12 Feb. 1877.

128.   The durbar: *Amrita Bazar Patrika*, 1 Feb. 1877; *Bharat Sangskarak*, 5 Feb. 1877, RNN.

128–9.   Deaths in Noakhali and Chittagong: Porch to Lowis, 9 Apr. 1877, 134–5; Lowis to Secy to Financial Dept, 27 Apr. 1877, FDP/M [May 1877], 3–7; Junior Secy to GoB to Lowis, 4 May 1877, in *Papers on the Subject of the Bengal Cyclone* (1877), 85; Memo by Lowis, 18 Apr. 1877, FDP/M [May 1877], 143–4; *Hindoo Patriot*, 12 Feb. 1877.

129.   Deaths in Bakarganj: Barton to Peacock, 16 Mar. 1877 [Apr. 1877], 120–2; Peacock to Secy to GoB, 24 Mar. 1877 [Apr. 1877], 118–20.

129–30.   Revised estimate: Resolution of the GoB, 27 March 1877, in *Papers on the Subject of the Bengal Cyclone* (1877), 70–1. The Chittagong correspondent to the *Hindoo Patriot*, 27 Nov. 1876, mentions a British official who reported only as many deaths as he saw corpses in the neighbourhood, putting local estimates that included the numbers swept away down to exaggeration.

130.   Commissioners' reports: Peacock to Secy to GoB, 24 Mar. 1877 [Apr. 1877], 118–20; Junior Secy to GoB to Peacock, 2 Apr. 1877, 127; Memo by Lowis, 18 Apr. 1877, FDP/M [May 1877], 143–4.

6. THE AFTERMATH

133.   Bakarganj correspondent: Quoted in the *Hindoo Patriot*, 15 Jan. 1877.

133–4.   Act of providence: *Hindoo Patriot*, 27 Nov. 1876.

134–5.   Rent dispute: Porch to Inspector-General of Police, 7 May 1877, NDR 84, 48–51; Porch to Political Agent of Hill Tippera, 15 Nov. 1876, NDR 80, 191–2; Porch to Sarkar & Supt of Police, 17 Nov. 1876, NDR 80, 199–200; Porch to Lyons, 1 Dec. 1876, NDR 80,

268; Porch to Sarkar, 4 Dec. 1876, NDR 80, 275; Porch to Inspector-General of Police, 7 May 1877, NDR 84, 48–51; Porch to Supt of Police, 26 June 1877, NDR 84, 161–3; Porch to Lowis, 31 Oct. 1877, NDR 81, 343–7.

135.   Advances: Pellew to Porch, 6 Dec. 1876 [Jan. 1877], 7–9; Pellew to Porch, 8 Dec. 1876 [Jan. 1877], 9–11.

135–6.   Manpura and Chota Basdia: Peacock to Secy to Financial Dept, 8 Jan. 1877, 17; Barton to Peacock, 26 Mar. 1877 [Apr. 1877], 133.

136.   Noakhali: Porch to Lowis, 3 Apr. 1877, 135–6.

136.   Remission and suspension: Smith to Secy to GoB, 12 Nov. 1876, 175–6; FDP/M, B series, June 1877, 149–50, 153–4, 169.

137.   Government estates: Barton to Peacock, 7 Jan. 1877 [Feb. 1877], 41–5; FDP/M, B Series, July 1877, 170–2; Porch to Lowis, 3 Apr. 1877, 135–6.

137–9.   Temple and the Madras famine: William Digby, *The Famine Campaign in Southern India*, ii (1878), 55–9, 397–405; Davis, *Late Victorian Holocausts* (2001), 37–41.

139–40.   Bengali newspapers: *Amrita Bazar Patrika*, 25 Jan. 1877; *Bharat Sangskarak*, 29 Jan. 1877, RNN; *Hindu Hitoishini*, 17 Mar. 1877, RNN; *Sadharani*, 25 Mar. 1877, RNN; *Bharat Mihir*, 5 Apr. 1877, RNN.

140.   Results of Temple's policy: Davis, *Late Victorian Holocausts* (2001), 37–41.

140.   Famine in Chittagong: *Samaj Darpan*, 15 June 1877, RNN; *Grambarta Prakashika*, 23 June 1877, RNN.

141.   Criticisms of government's attitude: *Grambarta Prakashika*, 23 June 1877, RNN; *Amrita Bazar Patrika*, 21 June 1877.

141–2.   Worsening situation: *Soma Prakash*, 13 Aug. 1877, RNN; *Sadharani*, 26 Aug. 1877, RNN.

142.   'Disloyalty' of press: *Sambad Prabhakar*, 20 Aug. 1877, RNN; *Hindu Hitoishini*, 1 Sept. 1877, RNN; *Dacca Prakash*, 2 Sept. 1877, RNN.

142–3.   Vernacular Press Act: Buckland, *Bengal Under the Lieutenant-Governors*, ii (1901), 713–18.

143.   Relocation of headquarters: Peacock to Secy to GoB, 19 Nov. 1876, 189–95.

143–4.   Dutt's background and appointment: Gupta, *Life and Work of Romesh Chunder Dutt* (1911), 17–22, 40–4.

144–5.   Dutt's recommendations: Dutt to Barton, 15 Apr. 1877, FDP/M [May 1877], 147–9.

145–6.   Proposal to distribute rice: Dutt to Barton, 30 May 1877, FDP/M [June 1877], 166–7.

146.   Barton's response: Barton to Peacock, 1 June 1877, FDP/M, 165–6.

146–7.   Further inquiries and explanation: Dutt to Barton, 5 June 1877, FDP/M, 170–1.

147.   Barton's continued reluctance: Barton to Peacock, 6 June 1877, FDP/M, 170.

147–8.   Relief centres: Dutt to Barton, 21 June 1877, FDP/M [July 1877], 3–5; Peacock to Secy to Financial Dept, 3 July 1877, FDP/M, 7–8; Peacock to Secy to Financial Dept, 18 July 1877, FDP/M, 8; Dutt to Barton, 19 July 1877, FDP/M, 11–13.

148.   Social differences: Beveridge, *The District of Bakarganj* (1876), 156, 171.

148–9.   Final report: Dutt to Barton, 19 July 1877, FDP/M, 11–13.

149.   Return to Bakarganj: Gupta, *Life and Work of Romesh Chunder Dutt* (1911), 44.

149.   Economic nationalism: Dutt, *India in the Victorian Age* (1904), xvii–xix; *The Economic History of India Under Early British Rule* (1906). In *India in the Victorian Age*, vi–viii, Dutt uses the recovery of Dakhin Shahbazpur after the cyclone as an example of the prosperity of eastern Bengal (which escaped the great famines of the nineteenth century) in relation to other parts of India. Yet as the earlier chapters of this book have shown, that prosperity was subject to several qualifications—not least the risk of being drowned by a storm-wave.

149–50. Law and order in Noakhali: Porch to Supt of Police, 5 Apr. 1877, NDR 83, 249–51; *Report on the Administration of Criminal Justice* (1878), 2–3; *Report on the Administration of Criminal Justice* (1879), 4–6.

150. Chittagong: *Report on the Administration of Criminal Justice* (1878), 3; *Report on the Administration of Criminal Justice* (1879), 4; *Sadharani*, 26 Aug. 1877, RNN.

150–1. Bakarganj: *Report on the Administration of Criminal Justice* (1878), 2–5; Peacock to Secy to Judicial Dept, 24 June 1878, HDP/J, NAI; Secy to Judicial Dept to Peacock, 6 July 1878, HDP/J, NAI; Peacock to Secy to Judicial Dept, 13 July 1878, HDP/J, NAI.

151. Deputy inspector-general's report: Dy Inspector-General of Police to Inspector-General of Police, Lower Provinces, 12 July 1878, HDP/J, NAI.

151–2. Inspector-general's report and recommendation: Monro to Secy to Judicial Dept, 13 Sept. 1878, HDP/J, NAI.

152. Eden's comments: Secy to Judicial Dept to Monro, 9 Oct. 1878, HDP/J, NAI; Secy to Judicial Dept to Peacock, 9 Oct. 1878, HDP/J, NAI.

153. Barton's defence: Memorandum on Police Administration in Bengal, 4 Mar. 1879, HDP/J, NAI.

153. Temple's opinion: Minute by Temple, 21 Nov. 1876, 151–7.

153–4. Raised houses: *The Times*, 29 Nov. 1876; Gupta to Barton, 22 Nov. 1876, 199–200.

154. Mounds: Rainey to Secy to Financial Dept, 12 Jan. 1877, 23–4.

154–5. Sagar Island: Gomess to Commissioner of Revenue, Dacca Division, 7 Dec. 1876 [Jan. 1877], 21–2; Gomess to Secy to Board of Revenue, 20 Feb. 1877, FDP/M [May 1877], 151.

155. Pellew's opinion: Pellew to Secy to GoB, 17 Feb. 1877, 38–9.

155–6. Earlier protective works: Elliott, *Report of the Vizagapatam and Backergunge Cyclones* (1877), 169.

156. Inquiry ordered: Junior Secy to GoB to Peacock and Lowis, 18 Jan. 1877, 25.

156–7. Bakarganj inquiry: Barton to Peacock, 12 Mar. 1877 [Apr. 1877], 130–1.

157. Noakhali inquiry: Porch to Lowis, 16 Feb. 1877, NDR 81, 141; Porch to Lowis, 1 Apr. 1877, NDR 81, 176–7.

158. Government's resolution: Ascoli, *A Revenue History of the Sundarbans* (1921), 66–7.

158. 'Fatal forgetfulness': *The Times*, 5 Jan. 1877.
158. Traditional warnings: Howell, 'Indigenous Early Warning Indicators of Cyclones' (2003), 5; Elliott, *Report of the Vizagapatam and Backergunge Cyclones* (1877), 145.
158–9. Scientific warnings: *The Times*, 3 Jan. 1877.
159. Strachey's response: *The Times*, 6 Jan. 1877.
159. Elliott's view: Elliott to Secy to Financial Dept, 16 Feb. 1877 [Mar. 1877], 91–2.
159–60. Existing system: Blanford, *Report of the Meteorological Reporter to the Government of Bengal* (1868), 1–6.
160. Official inaction: *The Times*, 3 Jan. 1877.
161. 1881 census: Bourdillon, *Report on the Census of Bengal* (1883), 45–7, 56–7.
161. 1891 census in Bakarganj: O'Donnell, *Census of India* (1893), 78–9.
161–2. 1891 census in Noakhali: O'Donnell, *Census of India* (1893), 80–1; 'Report on the Census of the District of Noakhali', 1891, DCRR Noakhali, 4–5.
162–3. Cadastral survey: A search of the local record rooms in Noakhali and Chittagong suggests that the volumes for those districts have not been preserved. The Bakarganj survey records (known as 'mouza notes') are organised by village, and include information on revenue and rent, topography, crops, markets, communications, tenures, the composition of the population, relations between landlords and tenants, notable murders and riots, and local legends. The examples given here are from the volumes for Bauphal, ii, RS 1893, and Barhanuddin, RS 1711, 1830, 1727, 1818, 1812, 1731, 1823.
163–4. Sundarbans policy: Pargiter, 'Cameos of Indian Districts' (1889), 299; Jack, *Final Report* (1915), 123.

EPILOGUE: THE TRIAL

165–6. The trial: This sequence is based on Nagendra Ray's poem *Pabaner Otyachar* (The Terror of a Storm); the poem was written shortly after the 1876 cyclone and published that year in Barisal.

BIBLIOGRAPHY

MANUSCRIPT COLLECTIONS

West Bengal State Archives, Calcutta

Presidency Commissioner Sundarbans Records, 1829–58
Controller of Salt Chaukis Records, 1846–58
Financial Department Proceedings, 1876–77
Statistical Department Proceedings, 1873

National Archives of Bangladesh, Dhaka

Noakhali District Records, 1876–77
'History of Kutubdia', 1934

Deputy Commissioner's Record Room, Barisal

Mouza Notes for Bauphal, Patuakhali, and Barhanuddin

Deputy Commissioner's Record Room, Noakhali

'Report on the Census of the District of Noakhali', 1891

National Archives of India, New Delhi

'Extract from Mr. R. Knox's Field Book of a Survey of the Islands between
  the Chittagong Coast and the Eastern Side of the Sunderbunds', 1803
Historical Maps of the Survey of India
MRIO-Miscellaneous Maps of the Survey of India
Reports on Native Newspapers, Bengal, 1876–77

BIBLIOGRAPHY

Home Department Proceedings, 1878–79

India Office Records, British Library, London
Public and Judicial Department Records, 1867

Angus Library and Archive, Oxford
Annual Reports of the Committee of the Baptist Missionary Society, 1875–78

HOUSE OF COMMONS PARLIAMENTARY PAPERS

Report from the Select Committee on Salt, British India, Together with the Minutes of Evidence, and Appendix (1836).

Report of the Commissioner Appointed to Inquire into and Report upon the Manufacture and Sale of, and Tax upon Salt in British India, and More Especially upon the Practicability of Substituting for Present Arrangements, a System of Excise in the Presidencies of Bengal and Madras (1856).

Report from the Select Committee on East India Finance, Together with the Proceedings of the Committee, Minutes of Evidence, and Appendix (1871).

Papers on the Subject of the Bengal Cyclone and Storm-Wave of the 31st October to 1st November 1876, and the Subsequent Cholera Epidemic (1877).

NEWSPAPERS AND PERIODICALS

Amrita Bazar Patrika (Calcutta)
The Bengalee (Calcutta)
Bengal Times (Dacca)
The Economist (London)
Friend of India (Calcutta)
Hindoo Patriot (Calcutta)
Missionary Herald (London)
The Times (London)

PUBLISHED WORKS

Ahmed, Rafiuddin, *The Bengal Muslims 1871–1906: A Quest for Identity* (Delhi, 1981).

BIBLIOGRAPHY

Allen, C.G.H., *Final Report on the Survey and Settlement of the District of Chittagong, 1888 to 1898* (Calcutta, 1900).

Ambirajan, S., *Classical Political Economy and British Policy in India* (Cambridge, 1978).

Amrith, Sunil, *Crossing the Bay of Bengal: The Furies of Nature and the Fortunes of Migrants* (Cambridge, Mass., 2013).

Arnold, David, 'Famine in Peasant Consciousness and Peasant Action: Madras 1876–8', in Ranajit Guha, ed., *Subaltern Studies III: Writings on South Asian History and Society* (Delhi, 1984), 62–115.

—— 'Cholera and Colonialism in British India', *Past & Present*, 113 (1986), 118–51.

—— *Science, Technology and Medicine in Colonial India* (Cambridge, 2004).

—— 'Agriculture and "Improvement" in Early Colonial India: A Pre-History of Development', *Journal of Agrarian Change*, 5:4 (2005), 505–25.

Ascoli, F.D., *A Revenue History of the Sundarbans from 1870 to 1920* (Calcutta, 1921).

Bandyopadhyay, Manik, *The Boatman of the Padma* (1936; Hyderabad, 2012).

Banerjee, Rajendra Lal, *Agricultural Sayings in Bengal, with Analogous Sayings in Bihar and Orissa* (Calcutta, 1914).

Barui, Balai, *The Salt Industry of Bengal, 1757–1800: A Study in the Interaction of British Monopoly Control and Indigenous Enterprise* (Calcutta, 1985).

Basu, Pyari Mohan, *Survey and Settlement of the Dakhin Shahbazpur Estates in the District of Backergunge, 1889–1895* (Calcutta, 1896).

Beames, John, *Memoirs of a Bengal Civilian* (London, 1961).

Begum, Rasheda, 'Women in Environmental Disasters: The 1991 Cyclone in Bangladesh', *Focus on Gender*, 1:1 (1993), 34–9.

Bellew, H.W., *Cholera in India, 1862–1881: Bengal Province, 1862–1881, and Review* (Calcutta, 1884).

Beveridge, H., *The District of Bakarganj: Its History and Statistics* (London, 1876).

Beverley, Henry, *Report on the Census of Bengal, 1872* (Calcutta, 1872).

Bhattacharya, S., and B. B. Chaudhuri, 'Regional Economy (1757–1857):

Eastern India', in Dharma Kumar, ed., *The Cambridge Economic History of India, 1757–1970* (Cambridge, 1983), 270–332.

Blanford, H.F., *Report of the Meteorological Reporter to the Government of Bengal, for the Year 1867–68* (Calcutta, 1868).

——— 'Catalogue of the Recorded Cyclones in the Bay of Bengal up to the End of 1876', *Journal of the Asiatic Society of Bengal*, 46:2 (1877), 328–38.

Bose, Sugata, *Peasant Labour and Colonial Capital: Rural Bengal Since 1770* (Cambridge, 1993).

Bourdillon, J.A., *Report on the Census of Bengal, 1881* (Calcutta, 1883).

A Brief History of the Cyclone at Calcutta and Vicinity, 5th October 1864 (Calcutta, 1865).

Buchanan, Francis, *Francis Buchanan in Southeast Bengal (1798): His Journey to Chittagong, the Chittagong Hill Tracts, Noakhali, and Comilla*, ed. Willem van Schendel (Dhaka, 1992).

Buckland, C.E., *Bengal Under the Lieutenant-Governors*, 2 vols (Calcutta, 1901).

Campbell, George, *Memoirs of My Indian Career*, 2 vols (London, 1893).

Carey, William, 'Prospectus of an Agricultural and Horticultural Society in India', *The Monthly Magazine*, 51:352 (1821), 254–6.

Chakrabarti, Haribandhu, *Bapre Ki Bishom Jhor!* (Barisal, 1876).

Chattopadhyay, Basudeb, *Crime and Control in Early Colonial Bengal, 1770–1860* (Calcutta, 2000).

Chaudhuri, B.B., 'Agrarian Relations: Eastern India', in Dharma Kumar, ed., *The Cambridge Economic History of India, 1757–1970* (Cambridge, 1983), 86–177.

Chaudhuri, Nirad C., *Thy Hand, Great Anarch!: India 1921–1952* (London, 1990).

Dambeck, Carl, 'The Great Bengal Cyclone of 1876', *The Popular Science Monthly*, 12 (1877), 192–5.

Davis, Mike, *Late Victorian Holocausts: El Niño Famines and the Making of the Third World* (London, 2001).

Digby, William, *The Famine Campaign in Southern India*, 2 vols (London, 1878).

D'Souza, Rohan, *Drowned and Dammed: Colonial Capitalism and Flood Control in Eastern India* (New Delhi, 2006).

Dutt, Romesh Chunder, *India in the Victorian Age: An Economic History of the People* (London, 1904).

—— *The Economic History of India Under Early British Rule* (2nd edn, London, 1906).

Eaton, Richard M., *The Rise of Islam and the Bengal Frontier, 1204–1760* (New Delhi, 1994).

Elliott, J., *Report of the Vizagapatam and Backergunge Cyclones of October 1876* (Calcutta, 1877).

Gait, E.A., *Census of India, 1901, Volume VI: The Lower Provinces of Bengal and their Feudatories* (Calcutta, 1902).

Gastrell, J.E., *Geographical and Statistical Report of the Districts of Jessore, Fureedpore and Backergunge* (Calcutta, 1868).

—— and Henry F. Blanford, *Report on the Calcutta Cyclone of the 5th October 1864* (Calcutta, 1866).

Gilmour, David, *The Ruling Caste: Imperial Lives in the Victorian Raj* (London, 2005).

Grant, Charles, *Observations on the State of Society Among the Asiatic Subjects of Great Britain, Particularly with Respect to Morals, and on the Means of Improving It* (London, 1797).

Guha, Ramachandra, 'State Forestry and Social Conflict in British India', *Past & Present*, 123 (1989), 141–77.

Guha, Ranajit, *A Rule of Property for Bengal: An Essay on the Idea of Permanent Settlement* (2nd edn, Ranikhet, 2016).

Gupta, J.N., *Life and Work of Romesh Chunder Dutt, C.I.E.* (London, 1911).

Harrison, Henry Leland, *The Bengal Embankment Manual* (Calcutta, 1875).

Harrison, Mark, *Public Health in British India: Anglo-Indian Preventive Medicine, 1859–1914* (Cambridge, 1994).

Hooker, Joseph Dalton, *Himalayan Journals, or, Notes of a Naturalist in Bengal, the Sikkim and Nepal Himalayas, the Khasia Mountains, &c.*, 2 vols (London, 1854).

Hora, Sunder Lal, 'Worship of the Deities Ola, Jhola and Bon Bibi in Lower Bengal', *Journal of the Asiatic Society of Bengal*, 29:1 (1933), 1–4.

Hossain, Hameeda, 'The Alienation of Weavers: Impact of the Conflict Between the Revenue Department and Commercial Interests of the East

India Company, 1750–1800', *Indian Economic & Social History Review*, 16:3 (1979), 323–45.

Howell, Philippa, 'Indigenous Early Warning Indicators of Cyclones: Potential Application in Coastal Bangladesh', Disaster Studies Working Paper 6, Benfield Hazard Research Centre (2003).

Hunter, W.W., *A Statistical Account of Bengal*, 20 vols (London, 1875–7).

Iqbal, Iftekhar, *The Bengal Delta: Ecology, State and Social Change, 1840–1943* (Basingstoke, 2010).

Islam, Sirajul, *Rural History of Bangladesh: A Source Study* (Dhaka, 1977).

——— *The Permanent Settlement in Bengal: A Study of Its Operation, 1790–1819* (Dhaka, 1979).

——— *Bengal Land Tenure: The Origin and Growth of Intermediate Interests in the 19th Century* (Calcutta, 1988).

——— ed., *Banglapedia: National Encyclopedia of Bangladesh* (Dhaka, 2006).

Jack, J.C., *Final Report on the Survey and Settlement Operations in the Bakarganj District, 1900 to 1908* (Calcutta, 1915).

——— *Bakarganj* (Calcutta, 1918).

Jameson, James, *Report on the Epidemick Cholera Morbus: As it Visited the Territories Subject to the Presidency of Bengal, in the Years 1817, 1818 and 1819* (Calcutta, 1820).

Jarrett, H.S., *The Ain i Akbari*, ii (Calcutta, 1891).

Karim, Abdul, *Murshid Quli Khan and His Times* (Dacca, 1963).

Kidd, Joseph, *Directions for the Homeopathic Treatment of Cholera* (London, 1866).

Klein, Ira, 'Imperialism, Ecology and Disease: Cholera in India, 1850–1950', *Indian Economic & Social History Review*, 31:4 (1994), 491–518.

Macnamara, C., *A History of Asiatic Cholera* (London, 1876).

Marshall, P.J., *Bengal: The British Bridgehead: Eastern India 1740–1828* (Cambridge, 1987).

Metcalf, Thomas R., *Ideologies of the Raj* (Cambridge, 1995).

Mitra, Debendra Bijoy, *The Cotton Weavers of Bengal, 1757–1833* (Calcutta, 1978).

Mukerjee, Radhakamal, *The Changing Face of Bengal: A Study in Riverine Economy* (Calcutta, 1938).

Murray, John, *Report on the Treatment of Epidemic Cholera* (Calcutta, 1869).

The Mutlah as an Auxiliary Port to Calcutta: Its Progress and Prospects (Calcutta, 1858).

Nakazato, Nariaki, *Agrarian System in Eastern Bengal, c. 1870–1910* (Calcutta, 1994).

Noma, Haruo and Ratan Lal Chakraborty, eds, *Agricultural and Rural Development in Bangladesh: Select Records on Agriculture, Land Revenue, Economy and Society of Noakhali District, 1849–1878* (Dhaka, 1990).

O'Donnell, C.J., *The Black Pamphlet of Calcutta: The Famine of 1874* (London, 1876).

—— *Census of India, 1891, Volume III: The Lower Provinces of Bengal and their Feudatories* (Calcutta, 1893).

O'Malley, L.S.S., *Chittagong* (Calcutta, 1908).

Palit, Chittabrata, *Tensions in Bengal Rural Society: Landlords, Planters and Colonial Rule, 1830–1860* (Calcutta, 1975).

Pargiter, F.E., 'Cameos of Indian Districts: The Sundarbans', *Calcutta Review*, 89:178 (1889), 280–301.

—— *A Revenue History of the Sundarbans from 1765 to 1870* (Calcutta, 1885; repr. Alipore, 1934).

Pellew, F.H., 'Physical Characteristics of Backergunge', *Calcutta Review*, 39:78 (1864), 199–209.

Phillips, Arthur, *The Law Relating to the Land Tenures of Lower Bengal* (Calcutta, 1876).

Piddington, Henry, *The Sailor's Horn-Book for the Law of Storms: Being a Practical Exposition of the Theory of the Law of Storms, and its Uses to Mariners of All Classes in All Parts of the World* (London, 1848).

—— *A Letter to the Most Noble James Andrew, Marquis of Dalhousie, Governor General of India, on the Storm-Waves of the Cyclones in the Bay of Bengal, and their Effects in the Sunderbunds* (Calcutta, 1853).

Pogson, Robert, *Captain Pogson's Narrative During a Tour to Chateegaon, 1831* (Serampore, 1831).

Prain, D., *Flora of the Sundribuns* (Calcutta, 1903).

Principal Heads of the History and Statistics of the Dacca Division (Calcutta, 1868).

Proceedings of the Asiatic Society of Bengal (Calcutta, 1868).

BIBLIOGRAPHY

Rangarajan, Mahesh, and K. Sivaramakrishnan, eds, *India's Environmental History: Colonialism, Modernity, and the Nation* (Ranikhet, 2012).

Ray, Nagendra, *Pabaner Otyachar* (Barisal, 1876).

Raychaudhuri, Tapan, 'Permanent Settlement in Operation: Bakarganj District, East Bengal', in Robert E. Frykenberg, ed., *Land Control and Social Structure in Indian History* (Madison, 1969), 163–74.

——— *The World in Our Time: A Memoir* (New Delhi, 2011).

Rennell, James, *A Bengal Atlas: Containing Maps of the Theatre of War and Commerce on that Side of Hindoostan* (London, 1781).

——— *Memoir of a Map of Hindoostan, or the Mogul Empire* (3rd edn, London, 1793).

——— *The Journals of Major James Rennell, First Surveyor-General of India, Written for the Information of the Governors of Bengal During his Surveys of the Ganges and Brahmaputra Rivers, 1764 to 1767*, ed. T.H.D. La Touche (Calcutta, 1910).

Report of the Committee of the Cyclone Relief Fund of 1867 (Calcutta, 1868).

Report on the Administration of Bengal (Calcutta, 1876–80).

Report on the Administration of Criminal Justice in the Lower Provinces of Bengal (Calcutta, 1878–79).

Report on the Condition of the Lower Classes of Population in Bengal (Calcutta, 1888).

Roy, Tirthankar, *The Economic History of India, 1857–1947* (New Delhi, 2000).

——— *Natural Disasters and Indian History* (New Delhi, 2012).

Schwartz, Stuart B., *Sea of Storms: A History of Hurricanes in the Greater Caribbean from Columbus to Katrina* (Princeton, 2015).

Sen, Amartya, *Poverty and Famines: An Essay on Entitlement and Deprivation* (Oxford, 1981).

Sen, Romesh Chandra, *Final Report on the Minor Settlement Operations in the District of Noakhali, 1928–1936* (Calcutta, 1939).

Serajuddin, A.M., 'The Salt Monopoly of the East India Company's Government in Bengal', *Journal of the Economic and Social History of the Orient*, 21:3 (1978), 304–22.

Sinha, D., *Purbabanger Kobigaan* (Calcutta, 1993).

Steinberg, Ted, *Acts of God: The Unnatural History of Natural Disaster in America* (2nd edn, New York, 2006).

BIBLIOGRAPHY

Sunder, D.H.E., *The Mughs of the Sundarbans, Backergunge District* (Calcutta, 1903).

Taylor, James, *A Sketch of the Topography & Statistics of Dacca* (Calcutta, 1840).

Temple, Richard, *Men and Events of My Time in India* (London, 1882).

────── *The Story of My Life*, 2 vols (London, 1896).

Thompson, W.H., *Final Report on the Survey and Settlement Operations in the District of Noakhali, 1914 to 1919* (Calcutta, 1919).

Webster, J.E., *Noakhali* (Allahabad, 1911).

Westland, J., *A Report on the District of Jessore: Its Antiquities, Its History, and Its Commerce* (Calcutta, 1871).

Wise, James, *Notes on the Races, Castes, and Trades of Eastern Bengal* (London, 1883).

ACKNOWLEDGEMENTS

I am grateful to Sekhar Bandyopadhyay for his valuable advice on this project, and to Pauline Keating for her interest and encouragement. I also wish to thank David Arnold, James Beattie, and Richard Hill; Kamalika Mukherjee, Sraman Mukherjee, and Ritwika Misra; Protima Roychowdhury and the Bigyanananda Mission; Rachna Singh and Mahesh Gopalan; Azizul Rasel and Rumana Sharmin, Rubayet Simin, and Shariful Islam; Nayeem Wahra, Coast Trust, and Sangkalpa Trust; Sharif Uddin Ahmed, Sirajul Islam, Ahmed Kamal, and Muntassir Mamoon; Utathya Chattopadhyaya, Rohan D'Souza, Iftekhar Iqbal, Emily O'Gorman, Mahesh Rangarajan, Tirthankar Roy, and Willem van Schendel; Michael Dwyer, Farhaana Arefin, Sebastian Ballard, and Daisy Leitch; the people of the coast who spoke to me about their experience of cyclone disasters; the staff of the archives, libraries, and record rooms in which I carried out my research; and, for financial assistance, Victoria University of Wellington and the New Zealand India Research Institute.

INDEX